CAMBRIDGE LIBRAR

Books of enduring scho

CW00468013

Women's Wr

The later twentieth century saw a huge wave of academic interest in women's writing, which led to the rediscovery of neglected works from a wide range of genres, periods and languages. Many books that were immensely popular and influential in their own day are now studied again, both for their own sake and for what they reveal about the social, political and cultural conditions of their time. A pioneering resource in this area is Orlando: Women's Writing in the British Isles from the Beginnings to the Present (http://orlando.cambridge.org), which provides entries on authors' lives and writing careers, contextual material, timelines, sets of internal links, and bibliographies. Its editors have made a major contribution to the selection of the works reissued in this series within the Cambridge Library Collection, which focuses on non-fiction publications by women on a wide range of subjects from astronomy to biography, music to political economy, and education to prison reform.

Guide to Windermere

Described by George Eliot as 'the only English woman that possesses thoroughly the art of writing', Harriet Martineau held a prominent position in the intellectual life of Victorian culture. This 1854 guide to Windermere was the first in her series of guides to the Lake District, leading eventually to her hugely successful *Complete Guide to the English Lakes*. In this *Guide*, Martineau engages with the emerging industry of literary tourism, and describes why the thriving village of Windermere warranted a 'new guide book'. She appreciatively details the natural features of the district and its architecture, and presents accounts of scenic walks and day tours to the neighbouring lakes, combining practical information with literary passages of description. An outstanding woman of her time, Martineau followed in Wordsworth's footsteps through imaginative empathy with the local landscape of the Lake District, continuing its rich literary associations. For more information on this author, see http://orlando.cambridge.org/public/ svPeople?person_id=martha

Cambridge University Press has long been a pioneer in the reissuing of out-of-print titles from its own backlist, producing digital reprints of books that are still sought after by scholars and students but could not be reprinted economically using traditional technology. The Cambridge Library Collection extends this activity to a wider range of books which are still of importance to researchers and professionals, either for the source material they contain, or as landmarks in the history of their academic discipline.

Drawing from the world-renowned collections in the Cambridge University Library, and guided by the advice of experts in each subject area, Cambridge University Press is using state-of-the-art scanning machines in its own Printing House to capture the content of each book selected for inclusion. The files are processed to give a consistently clear, crisp image, and the books finished to the high quality standard for which the Press is recognised around the world. The latest print-on-demand technology ensures that the books will remain available indefinitely, and that orders for single or multiple copies can quickly be supplied.

The Cambridge Library Collection will bring back to life books of enduring scholarly value (including out-of-copyright works originally issued by other publishers) across a wide range of disciplines in the humanities and social sciences and in science and technology.

Guide to Windermere

*With Tours to the Neighboring Lakes and
Other Interesting Places*

HARRIET MARTINEAU

CAMBRIDGE
UNIVERSITY PRESS

CAMBRIDGE UNIVERSITY PRESS

Cambridge, New York, Melbourne, Madrid, Cape Town, Singapore,
São Paolo, Delhi, Dubai, Tokyo

Published in the United States of America by Cambridge University Press, New York

www.cambridge.org
Information on this title: www.cambridge.org/9781108018357

© in this compilation Cambridge University Press 2010

This edition first published 1854
This digitally printed version 2010

ISBN 978-1-108-01835-7 Paperback

ACROSS THE HEAD OF STOCKGHYLL.

GUIDE

TO

WINDERMERE,

WITH

TOURS TO THE NEIGHBOURING LAKES AND OTHER
INTERESTING PLACES,

BY MISS HARRIET MARTINEAU.

With a Map,

AND ILLUSTRATIONS FROM DRAWINGS BY T. L. ASPLAND,
ENGRAVED BY W. J. LINTON.

TO WHICH ARE ADDED EXCURSIONS TO AND FROM KESWICK;

ALSO AN ACCOUNT OF THE

FLOWERING PLANTS, FERNS AND MOSSES

OF THE DISTRICT,

AND A COMPLETE DIRECTORY TO WINDERMERE AND ITS
NEIGHBOURHOOD.

WINDERMERE: — JOHN GARNETT.
LONDON: — WHITTAKER AND CO.

INDEX.

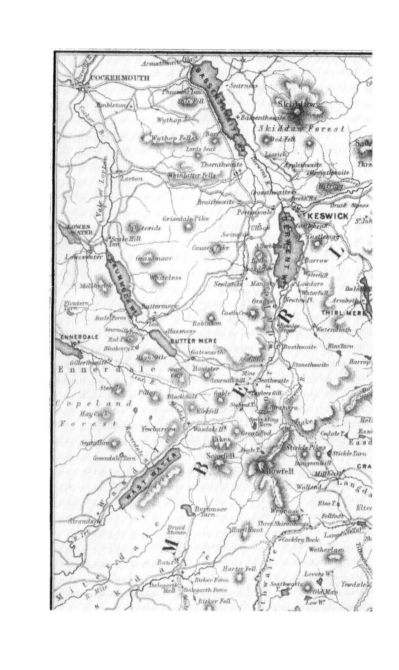

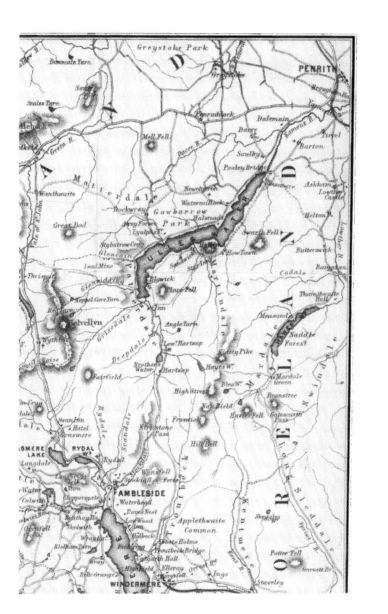

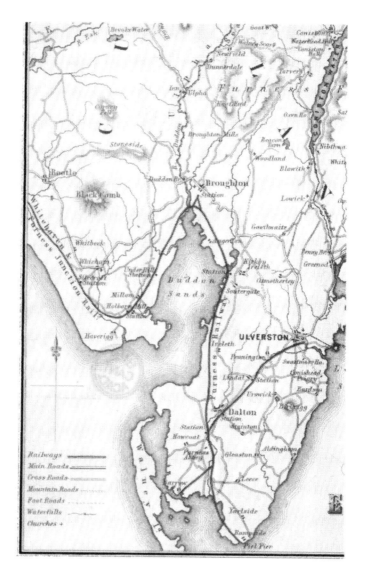

Railways
Main Roads
Cross Roads
Mountain Roads
Foot Roads
Waterfalls
Churches +

Published by John

MAP OF THE ENGLISH LAKES.

Scale of Miles

Willm Banks, Engraver, Edin^r

. Garnet, Windermere .

GUIDE TO WINDERMERE.

A few years ago there was only one meaning to the word WINDERMERE. It then meant a lake lying among mountains, and so secluded that it was some distinction even for the travelled man to have seen it. Now, there is a Windermere Railway Station, and a Windermere post office and hotel; — a thriving village of Windermere and a populous locality. This implies that a great many people come to the spot; and the spot is so changed by their coming, and by other circumstances, that a new guide book is wanted; for there is much more to point out than there used to be; and what used to be pointed out now requires a wholly new description. Such new guidance and description we now propose to give.

The traveller arrives, we must suppose, by the railway from Kendal, having been dropped at the Oxenholme Junction by the London train from the south, or the Edinburgh and Carlisle train from the north.

The railways skirt the lake district, but do not, and cannot, penetrate it: for the obvious reason that railways cannot traverse or pierce granite mountains or span broad lakes. If the time should ever come when iron roads will intersect the mountainous parts of Westmorland and Cumberland, that time is not yet; nor is it in view, — loud as have been the lamentations of some residents, as if it were to happen to-morrow. No one who has ascended Dunmail Raise, or visited the head of Coniston Lake, or gone by Kirkstone to Patterdale, will for a moment imagine that any conceivable railway will carry strangers over those passes, for generations to come. It is a great thing that steam can now convey travellers round the outskirts of the district, and up to its openings. This is now effectually done: and it is all that will be done by the steam locomotive during the lifetime of anybody yet born. The most important of the openings thus reached is that of WINDERMERE.

The mountain region of Cumberland and Westmorland has for its nucleus the cluster of tall mountains, of which Scawfell and Bowfell are the highest. *There* are the loftiest peaks and deepest valleys. These are surrounded by somewhat lower ridges and shallower vales; and these again by others, till the uplands are mere hills and the valleys scarcely sunk at all. It is into these exterior undulations that the railways penetrate; and, at the first ridge of any steepness, they must stop. It is this which decides the termination of the Windermere railroad, and which prevents the lateral railways from coming nearer than the outer base of the hills on the east and the coast on the west. When the traveller on foot or horseback sees certain reaches of Lake Windermere from Orrest Head, lying deep down below him, he knows he is coming near the end of the railway, which cannot yet plunge and climb as our old mail roads must do, if they exist here at all. As a general rule, lakes should be approached from the foot, that the ridges may rise, instead of sinking, before the observer's eye. But, so happy is the access to Windermere from the station, that it is hard to say that it could have been better ; and that access is, not from the south to its lower end, but from the south-east to about its middle. The old coach road over Orrest Head and the railway meet at the new village of Windermere, whence the road to Bowness descends, winding, for about a mile and a half, striking the shore at a point rather more than half way up the lake, and commanding the group of mountains that cluster about its head.

Supposing that the traveller desires to see the Windermere scenery thoroughly, we shall divide our directions into portions ; first exhibiting what is to be seen in the immediate neighbourhood of the Windermere Hotel, or within a moderate walk ; and then describing three tours, two of which may be easily taken in a day. One mountain trip will be added, and, these being faithfully prosecuted, the tourist may be assured that he has seen all that falls within the scope of a summer visitor.

A few minutes will take him to Orrest Head, where he will see a lovely view, — a picturesque cottage roof,

surrounded by trees, in the foreground ; grey rocks
cropping out of the sward on the other side of the
hedges; and in front, overlapping hills, range behind
range, with the grey waters of the lake lying below.
The hill to the right is part of the Elleray property, so
well known as the lake-home of Christopher North,
and now so much improved by its present proprietor,
Mr. Eastted. If the traveller should have the good
fortune to obtain a ticket of leave to enter the grounds,*
his first object should be to walk up that hill at
Elleray, by Mr. Eastted's new drive. All the way up,
the views are exquisite : but that from the summit,
— about 700 feet above the lake, is one of the
finest the district can show. The whole length of
Windermere extends below, with its enclosing hills
and wooded islands ; and towards the head, some of
the highest peaks and ridges may be seen : — Coniston
Old Man to the west ; Bowfell and the Langdale Pikes
to the northwest ; Fairfield to the north, with Loughrigg lying, as a mere dark ridge, across the head of

* A portion of the Elleray grounds are open to the public every
Monday and Friday. Tickets of admission, bearing date, are
issued on application to Mr. Garnett, at the Windermere Post-
office, by paying a small donation, not less than one shilling, for a
party of six persons, and, if above that number, the donation must
be doubled. The proceeds are for the benefit of the school for
the education of the poor, established by the Rev. J. A. Addison,
and the sick and aged poor of Windermere, who may need assistance. — Parties will enter at the gate opposite the post-office, and
proceed up the road to the right, which is the main road leading
to the top of the hill, and return by the same route. All branch
roads are strictly private.

Windermere; while, to the north-east, Troutbeck is disclosed, with its peaks of High Street and Hill Bell. All below are woods, with houses peeping out ; on a height of the opposite shore, Wray Castle; further north, the little Brathay Chapel, set down near the mouth of the valley; and between Loughrigg and the lake, at its head, the white houses of Clappersgate, with the chateau-like mansion of Croft Lodge conspicuous above the rest. This view is a good deal like the one from the hill behind the Windermere Hotel, which is reached by a lane turning off from Orrest Head. The Elleray one is the most extensive and complete to the north : but to enjoy the other, leave will be readily obtained at the hotel.

The village of Windermere is like nothing that is to be seen any where else. The new buildings (and all are new) are of the dark grey stone of the region, and are for the most part of a mediæval style of architecture. The Rev. J. A. Addison, of Windermere, has a passion for ecclesiastical architecture ; and his example has been a good deal followed. There is the little church of St. Mary, and there are the schools belonging to it, with their steep roofs of curiously-shaped slates : and there is St. Mary's Abbey, (new, in spite of its antique name), and St. Mary's Cottage. And there will be the new college of St. Mary, standing in a fine position, between the main road and the descent to the lake. This college, of which the Rev. J. A. Addison is the warden, is designed to afford a cheap and thorough education, on sound church principles, to the sons of clergymen chiefly, though not exclusively.

It is under high patronage, ecclesiastical and local.
The pupils, in a college garb of the olden time, are a
curious feature in the aspect of the place ; and they
will be more so when they get their new buildings to
live in. Judging by the plan and elevation put forth,
the edifice will be in excellent taste, and a great adornment to the neighbourhood. The large house, on the
hill and amidst the woods of the Elleray estate, as yet
unfinished, and often mistaken for the new college, is the
property of John Gandy, Esq., who has chosen a
charming site for his abode ; and a little further, on
the same side of the road, is the pretty villa-residence
of Miss Yates.

There are villas on either side the road, on almost
every favourable spot, all the way to Bowness. There
is to be a road past the college, leaving the present
one to be called by the inevitable title of "the old
road." We pass rows of lodging-houses ; and then
we see to the right the spot where the college is to be:
and to the left Ellerthwaite, the residence of Mr. Geo.
H. Gardner ; and then, to the right, the cottage of
Mylnbeck, the residence of the Misses Watson, daugh-
ters of the late bishop of Llandaff : a common house
in its aspect towards the road, but, as seen over the
wall, very pretty in its garden front. The next gate
on the left is the entrance to the Craig, built by Sir.
Thomas Pasley, and now inhabited by W. R. Greg,
Esq. Below this, the houses begin to thicken about
the entrance to Bowness. Among them, a road to the
left leads to one of the most charming points of view in
the neighbourhood, — a hill named Biscut How, crested

with rocks, which afford as fine a station as the summit of Elleray for a view of the entire lake and its
shores.

BOWNESS

Is the port of Windermere. There the new steamboats
put up; and thence go forth the greater number of
fishing and pleasure boats which adorn the lake. There
is a good deal of bustle in the place; and the lower
parts, near the water, are very hot in summer: and the
more since the building of a new lodging house in a
space near the church, which used to be called the lungs
of Bowness. The two great inns, however, are in airy
situations, — the garden platform of Ullock's Royal
Hotel overlooking the gardens that slope down to the
shore; and the Crown being on a hill which commands
the whole place. These inns are both extremely well
managed; and it is for the traveller to say whether
their charges, which are uniform, justify a complaint
which has been made, (we think unreasonably as
regards the Lake District in general) of high prices.
During the season, which extends from May to Novem-
ber, the charges are two shillings for breakfast, (including
meat, fish, &c.,) two shillings and sixpence for dinner;
and one shilling and sixpence for tea. A private sitting-
room is charged two shillings and sixpence per day.
Ullock's Hotel, called Royal since the visit of Queen
Adelaide in 1844, makes up between seventy and eighty
beds. Close at hand is a little museum, where the birds
of the district may be seen, exceedingly well stuffed
and arranged by Mr. Armstrong, a waiter at the hotel.
The Crown has ten private sitting rooms, and makes up

ninety beds. Nothing can well exceed the beauty of
the view from its garden seats.

The old churchyard of Bowness, with its dark yews,
and the weather-worn church, long and low, is the
most venerable object in the place. The chancel window of the church contains painted glass from Furness
Abbey. The tomb of Bishop Watson will be found in
the churchyard, near the east window. The rectory,
which is hardly less venerable than the church, stands
at a considerable distance from the village, and is
approached through fields and a garden. The old-
fashioned porch is there, of which this is said to be
the last remaining instance in the whole district, — the
roomy, substantial porch, with benches on each side,
long enough to hold a little company of parishioners,
and a round ivy-clad chimney immediately surmount-
ing the porch. Within, there is abundant space, with
little elevation; — plenty of room in the hall and
parlours, with ceilings that one can touch with the
hand. Almost every other noticeable edifice in Bowness is new, or at least modern; the schools, the gift of
the late Mr. Bolton of Storrs Hall, — the Italian villa,
called Belsfield, the property of the Baroness de Sternberg, and many others.

The visitor will first repair to the strand, to salute
the waters. He will find a good quay, with boats in
abundance, and several boat-houses within view. A
substantial little pier is built out into the lake; and
on either side is a steamboat moored during winter;
and to the end these two steamers come, six times a
day each, during the summer. To the right, gardens

slope down to this little bay; and they look gay even
in winter from their profusion of evergreens, and from
the ivy which clothes their walls. The church just
peeps out behind the houses above. Looking over the
lake, Curwen's island is just opposite. In May and
early June, the woods of that island, and of all the
promontories round, present a most diversified foliage,
— from the golden tufts of the oak to the sombre hue of
the pines, with every gradation of green between. In
July and August, the woods are what some call *too*
green, — massy and impenetrable, — casting deep shadows on the sward and the waters. Within the shadow
on the shore stands the angler, watching the dimpling
of the surface, as the fly touches it, or the fish leaps
from it : and within the shadow on the water, the boat
swings idly with the current; and the student, come
hither for recreation, reads or sleeps as he reclines,
waiting for the cool of the afternoon. Turning to the
north, the highest peaks are not seen from this strand;
but Fairfield and Loughrigg close in the head of the
lake.

Turning southwards along the margin, and walking
about a mile, the explorer reaches the point of the
promontory, Ferry Nab, which stretches out opposite
the Ferry House, — itself on the point of an opposite
promontory. There can hardly be a more charming
resting-place than a seat under the last trees of this
projection. It is breezy here ; and the waters smack the
shore cheerily. The Troutbeck hills here come into view,
and the head of the lake is grander. The round house
on Curwen's island is seen among the trees. The Ferry

house, under its canopy of tall sycamores, and with its
pebbly beach, is immediately opposite; and behind it
rises the wooded bank which is, in light or shadow, one
of the chief graces of the scene. If the sun shines
upon it, it is feathered with foliage to the very ridge,
and the bay beneath it is blue and lustrous. If the
sun has gone down behind it, the bay is black; and
every dipping bird sprinkles it with silver; and the
wild duck that comes sailing out with her brood, draws
behind her a pencil of white light. From this point,
a view opens to the south. In the expanse of waters
lies another island; and further down, on the eastern
shore, a pier extends with a little tower at the end.
This is Storrs: and at that pier did the guests embark
when Scott went to meet Canning at Mr. Bolton's, and
the fine regatta took place, (under the direction of
Christopher North) which is celebrated in Lockhart's
Life of Scott. This was only two years before Canning's
death, and seven before that of Scott. Mr. and Mrs.
Bolton are gone; and Christopher North himself has
lost all his health and vigour. The more reason that
the memory of that day should be preserved!

Instead of returning to his inn the way he came, the
stranger may make a moderate and pleasant walk by
going through Bowness on the Ambleside road, and
round by Cook's House. The first noticeable abode
that he will see is Rayrigg,—a rather low, rambling,
grey house, standing on the grass near a little bay of
the lake. It is a charming old-fashioned house, and its
position has every advantage, except that it stands too
low. On the high wall by the road side, immediately

WINDERMERE FROM NEAR STORRS.

before reaching the gate of Rayrigg, the stranger will be
struck with the variety of ferns. That wall is an excellent introduction to the stone fences of the region, —
richly adorned as many of them are with mosses and ferns.

Passing between woods, resounding with brawling
streams, the road leads up a rather steep ascent, the
summit of which is called Miller Brow. Hence is seen
what, in our opinion, is a view unsurpassed for beauty
in the whole Lake District. The entire lake lies below,
the white houses of Clappersgate being distinctly visible
at the north end and the Beacon at the south : and the
diversity of the framework of this sheet of water is
here most striking. The Calgarth woods, for which we
are indebted to Bishop Watson, rising and falling,
spreading and contracting below, with green undulating
meadows interposed, are a perfect treat to the eye ; and
so are the islands clustering in the centre of the lake.
Wray Castle stands forth well above the promontory
opposite ; and at the head, the Langdale Pikes, and
their surrounding mountains seem, in some states of
the atmosphere, to approach and overshadow the
waters ; and in others to retire, and shroud themselves
in soft haze and delicate hues peculiar to cloud land.
There is a new house, built just below the ridge at
Miller Brow by William Sheldon, which we have
thought, from the time the foundation was laid, the
most enviable abode in the country, — commanding a
view worthy of a mountain top, while sheltered by hill
and wood, and with the main road so close at hand that
the conveniences of life are as procurable as in a street.
A short descent hence brings the walker to Cook's

House, — the point where four roads meet. The one
to his left would˙ take him to Ambleside; the one
opposite, to Troutbeck. To reach his inn, he must take
the one to the right, which leads him straight home.

The next thing to be done is to take a survey of the
whole lake by a steamboat trip. During the summer,
two steamers make six trips each; so that the stranger
can choose his own hour, and go down or up first, as he
pleases. In accordance with the rule of lake approach,
we should recommend his going down first. He em-
barks at the pier at Bowness, and is carried straight
across to the Ferry, where the boats touch. Then the
course is southwards, with the lake narrowing, and the
hills sinking till the scenery becomes merely pretty.
The water is very shallow towards the foot, and the
practicable channel is marked out by posts. The
best work that the whole neighbourhood could
undertake would be the deepening of the lake at this
part, and of the river which carries off the overflow.
Not only is the passage of the steamers difficult: there
is a far worse evil in the inundations which take place
on all the low-lying lands, even up to Rydal, from
the insufficiency of the outlet. The mischief has much
increased since drainage has been introduced. The
excellent and indispensable practice of land drainage
must be followed up by an improvement in arterial
drainage, or floods are inevitable. The water which
formerly dribbled away in the course of many days, or
even weeks, now gushes out from the drains all at once;
and if the main outlets are not enlarged in proportion,
the waters are thrown back upon the land. This is the

case now in the neighbourhood of Windermere, — the
meadows and low-lying houses at Ambleside, a mile or
two from the lake, being flooded every winter by the
overflow of the lake first, then of the river, then of the
tributary streams. The Engineer Company gave fifty
pounds to have the lake deepened at Fell Foot, about
five years ago; and Mr. White, the proprietor of the
Newby Bridge Hotel, subscribed the same amount:
and this was good, as far as it went. But a far larger
operation is required. There is a weir below Newby
Bridge, to serve a corn mill. Now, the days of weirs
and watermills are coming to an end. In these days of
steam engines, it is not to be endured that hundreds of
acres should be turned into swamps, and hundreds of
lives lost by fever, ague, and rheumatism, for the sake
of a waterpower, which pays perhaps thirty pounds
or forty pounds a year. We say this of watermills
generally; and in regard to the need of sufficient arterial
drainage, we speak of the shores of Windermere in
particular. The expense of carrying off the utmost
surplus of the waters in the wettest season would be
presently repaid, here as anywhere else, by the improved
value of the land and house property, relieved from the
nuisance of flood.

The Swan Inn at Newby Bridge is exceedingly
comfortable; and the charges are very moderate. The
stranger will have to come again, on his way to Furness, at all events, and perhaps in some trip to Hawkshead; or when making the circuit of the lake by land.
Now, he merely calls for lunch or tea, during the
stopping of the steamer; and then he is off again, up

the lake. After the Ferry and Bowness, the next call is at Lowwood inn, where there are sure to be passengers landing or embarking. Between Bowness and Low-wood inn, Rayrigg has been seen, beside the little bay; and then Ecclerigg, with its overshadowing trees, and pretty pier. It is inhabited by Richard Luther Watson, Esq., nephew of the late Bishop of Llandaff. Just above Lowwood, high up on the wooded side of Wans-fell, will be seen Dove's Nest, once the abode of Mrs. Hemans, when its appearance was more primitive and less pretty than it is now, — improved as it has been by its present resident, her then young friend, the Rev. Robert Percival Graves. Next comes Wansfell Holme, inhabited by the Rev. James J. Hornby. This is another choice situation. On the opposite shore is Wray Castle, erected by James Dawson, Esq., — a most defensible-looking place for so peaceful a region; but an enviable residence, both from its interior beauty and the views it commands. Just above it, Pullwyke bay, where lily of the valley is found, runs far into the land; and overlooking it is seen Pull Cottage, the residence of Major Rogers. Next, the sweet, tranquil Brathay valley opens, with Mr. Redmayne's mansion of Brathay Hall, on a green slope above the lake; and just behind, on a wooded knoll in the gorge of the valley, the beautiful little church, called Brathay Chapel, built by Mr. Redmayne.

Two rivers fall into the lake, uniting just before they reach it : — the Rothay, which comes down from Dun-mail Raise, beyond Grasmere, and the Brathay, which issues from Elter Water, a group of pools, rather than a lake, lying at the foot of the hills near Langdale. The valleys of the Rothay and the Brathay are separated by Loughrigg, — the ridge which, at its further end, commands Grasmere. Its Windermere end shelters Clappersgate and Waterhead. The steamer sweeps round to the pier at Waterhead, where there is a cluster of dwellings, the most imposing of which is the large grey stone house called Wanlas How, the property of Alexander C. Brenchley, Esq. Omnibuses are in waiting here, from Ambleside and Grasmere, — the one, distant one mile; and the other, between five and six. Our tourist will, however, complete the circuit of the lake, by returning to Bowness.

There are plenty of boats to be had at Waterhead and Bowness, and watermen who are practiced and skilful. The stranger should be warned, however, against two dangers which it is rash to encounter. Nothing should induce him to sail on Windermere, or on any lake surrounded by mountains. There is no calculating on, or accounting for, the gusts that come down between the hills; and no skill and practice obtained by boating on rivers or the waters of a flat country are any sure protection here. And nothing should induce him to go out in one of the little skiffs which are too easily attainable here, and too tempting, from the ease of rowing them. The surface may become rough at any minute, and those skiffs are unsafe in all states of the water but the calmest. The long list of deaths occasioned in this way, — deaths both of residents and strangers, — should have put an end to the use of these light skiffs, long ago. The larger

boats are safe enough, and most skilfully managed by
their rowers : and the stranger can enjoy no better treat
than gliding along, for hours of the summer day, peeping into the coves and bays, coasting the islands, and
lying cool in the shadows of the woods.   The clearness
of the water is a common surprise to the resident in a
level country ; and it is pleasant sport to watch the
movements of the fish, darting, basking, or leaping in
the sunshine, or quivering their fins in the reflected ray.
What the quality of the trout and char is, the tourist
will probably find every day, at breakfast and dinner.

FIRST TOUR.

Of the three extended tours which we should advise
the stranger to take from his Windermere quarters,
that to Furness should be the first, because it traverses
the least mountainous parts of the district.

He will go down to Newby Bridge either by steamer,
or by the road, which passes the grounds of Storrs, and
cuts over hill and dale, and winds among the copses,
till it crosses the bridge, opposite the inn. It is eight
miles hence to the cheerful little town of Ulverstone,
which is now reached by the railway from Whitehaven;
and from Ulverstone, the railway stretches south, past
Furness Abbey, to the margin of the sea. From
Ulverstone to Furness, it is only seven miles. There
is a good inn, — (though not cheap, as cheapness is not
to be expected in the precincts of secluded ruins :) and
here the tourist should bespeak his bed, if he means to
study the Abbey.

The Abbey was founded in A.D. 1127. Its domains
extended over the whole promontory in which it lies,
and to the north, as far as the Shire Stones on Wrynose.
They occupied the space between Windermere on the
east and the Duddon on the west. The Abbot was a
sort of king; and his abbey was enriched, not only by

B

King Stephen, but by the gifts of neighbouring proprie-
tors, who were glad to avail themselves, not only of its
religious privileges, but of its military powers for the
defence of their estates against border foes, and the
outlaws of the mountains, — the descendants of the
conquered Saxons, who inherited their fathers' ven-
geance. The Abbey was first peopled from Normandy,
— a sufficient number of Benedictine monks coming
over from the monastery of Savigny to establish this
house in honour of St. Marye of Furnesse. In a few
years, their profession changed: they followed St.
Bernard, and wore the white cassock, caul and scapulary,
instead of the dress of the grey monks. It is strange
now to see the railway traversing those woods where
these grey-robed foreigners used to pass hither and
thither, on their holy errands to the depressed and
angry native Saxons dwelling round about. The situation of the Abbey, as is usual with religious houses, is
fine. It stands in the depth of a glen, with a stream
flowing by, — the sides of the glen being clothed with
wood. A beacon once belonged to it; a watch tower
on an eminence accessible from the Abbey, whose signal-
fire was visible all over Low Furness, when assistance
was required, or foes were expected. The building is of
the pale red stone of the district. It must formerly
have almost filled the glen: and the ruins give an
impression, to this day, of the establishment having
been worthy of the zeal of its founder, King Stephen,
and the extent of its endowments, which were princely.
The boundary-wall of the precincts inclosed a space of
sixty-five acres, over which are scattered remains that

have, within our own time, been interpreted to be those of the mill, the granary, the fish-ponds, the ovens and kilns, and other offices. As for the architecture, the heavy shaft is found alternating with the clustered pillar, and the round Norman with the pointed Gothic arch. The masonry is so good that the remains are, even now, firm and massive; and the winding staircases within the walls are still in good condition, in many places. The nobleness of the edifice consisted in its extent and proportions; for the stone would not bear the execution of any very elaborate ornament. The crowned heads of Stephen and his Queen Maude are seen outside the window of the Abbey, and are among the most interesting of the remains. It is all *triste* and silent now. The Chapter-house, where so many grave councils were held, is open to the babbling winds. Where the abbot and his train swept past in religious procession, over inscribed pavements, echoing to the tread, the stranger now wades among tall ferns and knotted grasses, stumbling over stones fallen from the place of honour. No swelling anthems are heard there now, or penitential psalms; but only the voice of birds, winds, and waters. But this blank is what the stranger comes for. Knowing what a territory the Abbots of Furness ruled over, like a kingdom, it is well to come hither to look how it is with that old palace and mitre, and to take one more warning of how Time shatters thrones, and dominations and powers, and causes the glories of the world to pass away.

The stranger will be among the ruins late, by moon or by star light; and again in the morning, before the dew is off, and when the hidden violet perfumes the area where the censer once was swung, and where the pillars cast long shadows on the sward. But he must not linger; for he has a good circuit to make before night.

The lake of Coniston, which is his next object, is in the district between Windermere and the Duddon, which has already been mentioned as formerly belonging to Furness Abbey. From Ulverstone, his road commands the estuary of the Leven for a few miles, and then approaches the foot of Coniston Water, which it reaches at eight miles from Ulverstone. Seven miles more bring him to the New Inn at Coniston, which, built under the direction of Mr. and Mrs. J. G. Marshall, is one of the most comfortable hotels in England. This lake, like Windermere, is flanked by low hills at the south end, and inclosed by magnificent mountains at the head, where Mr. J. G. Marshall's house and lands are more gloriously situated than almost any other in the region. The little town of Church Coniston, and the New Inn, are a mile short of Waterhead; and the stranger must stop, and look through the place, while his early dinner is preparing. The Old Man, eleventh in height of the mountains of the district, (2,576 feet) towers above him, and the abodes of the people will shew him that he is in the neighbourhood of a copper mine. There is one, some way up the mountain; and he may see the winding road up to it. Higher up, where there is an evident hollow, he is told that he would find a deep black tarn; and higher up, another. But to climb the mountain is a day's work, with much doubt of success, (that is, of a clear summit,) and he

CONISTON FROM BANK GROUND.

must to-day be satisfied with what is below. Yewdale,
with its grey rocks, cushioned with heather up to their
summits, stretches away northwards from the head of
the lake, into a gorge where the mountains overlap.
One of the crags there is called Raven Crag: and it is
said that a pair of ravens is living now, there or some-
where near. It is to be hoped that, now the eagles are
gone, the last ravens will not be destroyed or scared
away by the shot of the miners, or other rash sports-
men, who are too apt to bring down every bird they
see. There are many picturesque dwellings in the area
which is between the heights and the lake: but the
best view of these is from the point to which the
stranger will proceed, after his lunch or early dinner.
He must order his car to meet him in an hour at the
junction of the two lake roads, on the Hawkshead
road; and then he must walk a mile to the Waterhead,
and then on, round the head of the lake, in the direction
of Tent Lodge, which is seen nestling in its garden at
some elevation above the lake. The road passes the
site of the former Waterhead inn, now a young plantation of Mr. Marshall's. Then, commanding the whole
expanse of the lake, it begins to ascend, as it curves
round to the east; and, at about a mile and three-
quarters from the new inn, there stands the house in
which Elizabeth Smith lived and died; and, on the
opposite side of the road, Tent Lodge, built on the spot
where a tent was pitched, that she might draw her
dying breath with greater ease, and enjoy, as long as
possible, the incomparable landscape there stretched
before her. The boat-house is at the bottom of the

slope, down which she used to take her mother's guests;
and she and her sister were so well practiced at the oar
that they could show the beauties of the scene from
any point of the lake.   The finest station is, however,
from a field, — the first beyond the new house on
Coniston Bank.   Some people think this the finest view
in the whole district : and truly, the frequent visitor
pronounces it incomparable, every time he comes; and
the passing tourist feels that, once seen, it can never be
forgotten.   Nowhere else, perhaps, is the grouping of
the mountain peaks, and the indication of their recesses
so striking; and as to the foreground, with its glittering
waterfalls, its green undulations, its diversified woods,
its bright dwellings, and its clear lake, — it conveys the
strongest impression of joyful charm, — of fertility,
prosperity and comfort, nestling in the bosom of the
rarest beauty.

Retracing his steps for some way, and passing the
turn which would lead him down again to Tent Lodge,
the stranger has a rather steep ascent before him, from
point to point of which he finds, on looking behind
him, new views of the lake appearing, while the magni-
tude of the Old Man becomes more apparent as he
recedes from it.   By the roadpost, which indicates the
two ways to the two sides of the lake, he finds his car;
and then he proceeds through a wild country, — moorland, sprinkled with grey rock, — in the direction of
Hawkshead, which is three miles from Waterhead.

The parish church of Hawkshead is ancient; its
appearance is venerable; and it stands, as a church
should do, in full view of the country round, — of the

valley in which Esthwaite Water lies. Elizabeth Smith lies buried there ; and there is a tablet to her memory in the churchyard. At the ancient Grammar School of Hawkshead, Wordsworth and his brother were educated. Passing through the neat little town, the road turns to the left, to reach the northern end of Esthwaite Water, which is two miles long, and half a mile broad ; — a quiet sheet of water, with two promontories stretching into it, which appear like islands, nearly dividing it into a chain of ponds. Lakebank is a pretty place ; and further on, Lakefield, (J. R. Ogden's, Esq.,) at Near Sawrey, commands perhaps the best view in the valley. Just beyond, the road turns to the left, through an undulating country of considerable beauty. The view of Windermere from the highest point is very fine. The road leads through Farther Sawrey to the Ferry House. If there is daylight left, (and there may be, as the Ferry is only seven miles from Coniston Water-head) the traveller may as well go to the Station House, which he must have seen from the opposite side of the lake, peeping out of the ever-green woods. There he obtains fine views, up and down the lake, and may mark, on the way up, the largest laurels he has ever seen.

Meantime, the heavy, roomy ferry-boat is ready : the horse is taken out of the car ; and both are shipped. Two or three, or half a dozen people take advantage of the passage : the rowers, with their ponderous oars, are on the bench ; and the great machine is presently afloat. The Ferry House looks more tempting than ever when seen from under its own sycamores, — jutting

out as it does between quiet bays on either hand.   The
landing takes place on the opposite promontory : the
horse is put to, and the traveller ascends, through
Bowness, to his inn.   He is ready for his meal (be it
tea or supper) of lake trout or char.   The best char are
in Coniston Water : but they are good every where;
especially to hungry travellers, sitting at table within
sight of the waters whence they have just been fished.
The potted char of Coniston is sent, as every epicure
knows, to all parts of the world where men know what
is good.   As for the trout, there can be none finer
than that of Windermere.

SECOND TOUR.

BY TROUTBECK TO KIRKSTONE PASS AND PATTERDALE, AND
HOME BY AMBLESIDE.

The country people will tell the traveller, as he turns
up to Troutbeck at Cook's House, that he is going to
see "the handsomest view in these parts, — especially
at the back end of the year." And wonderfully fine
the views are, as the road ascends, commanding the
entire lake, and the whole range of mountains from
Coniston Old Man to Fairfield. The singular valley of
Troutbeck was once a wooded basin, where the terrified
Britons took refuge from the Romans, while the latter
were making their great road from Kendal to Penrith.
That road actually ran along the very ridge of the
Troutbeck hills, as any one may see who will climb the
mountain called, for this reason, High Street. What
a sight it must have been — the pioneers felling the
trees, and paving the way, and the soldiers following,
with their armour and weapons gleaming in the sun,
while the trembling natives cowered in the forest below,
— listening now to the blows of the workmen, and now
to the warlike music of the troops, marching up from
Kendal! After Romans and Saxons were gone, the
valley was a great park, and the inhabitants were
virtually serfs, in danger of the gallows, (which had a
hill to itself, named after it to this day) at the will

and pleasure of the one great man. In course of time, — that is, a good many centuries ago, — the valley was disparked, and divided among the inhabitants, — only one very large estate being left, — the new park, containing 2,000 acres. This was the estate given by Charles I, to Huddlestone Phillipson, for his services in the civil wars. The valley now contains a string of hamlets, — Town End, Town Head, High Green, Crag, and High Fold; and its farmsteads and outbuildings show some of the most curious specimens of ancient edifices that are to be seen in the district. Troutbeck is the most primitive of the frequented valleys of the district. To find any other so antique and characteristic, it is necessary to leave the high road, and explore the secluded dales of which the summer tourist sees and hears nothing. The dale looks from the uplands as if it had been scooped out between the ridges with a gigantic scoop. Its levels are parcelled out into small fields, of all manner of shapes; and the stream, — the *beck* abounding in *trout*, — winds along the bottom, from the foot of High Street, to fall into the lake just by Calgarth.

The road now followed by the tourist descends into the vale sharply, by the abode of John Wilson, Esq., at The How, and crosses the bridge, in full view of the chapel, which was consecrated in 1562, and thoroughly repaired in 1828. It is one of the small churches that, with their square tower and bell, look and sound so well in the dales. This one seats 160 worshippers. Immediately beyond the bridge, the road mounts again very steeply, till it joins that which runs along the hill

sides, on the western side of the valley. This road is
to be followed up the valley ; and the tourist must lose
none of its beauties. Behind him, there are views of
the receding lake, now diminished to the likeness of
a cabinet picture : — below is the deep vale with its
green levels : opposite the grassy slopes ascend to the
ridges of High Street and Hill Bell ; and before him,
Troutbeck Tongue protrudes, splitting the valley into
two, and being itself most lovely with its farmstead, and
dropped thorns, and coppice and grey rocks : while,
behind and above it, the vale head rises into grandeur,
with its torrents leaping down, and its pathway winding
up, indicating the pass into Mardale. The stranger is
not going that way, however. He turns over a gentler
pass to the left, which leads him, on the slope of Wansfell, away from Troutbeck. As he bids farewell to the
Tongue, he sees the summit of Kirkstone before him.
He is passing over the somewhat boggy upland where
the Stock takes its rise, to flow down to and through
Ambleside, after having taken the leap called Stockghyll
Force. The tourist may see that in the evening, if
there is time : — he is going the other way now.

His road meets the one from Ambleside at a small
public-house, which the Ordnance Surveyors have
declared the Highest Inhabited House in England :
and thus it is labelled by a board over the porch. In
clear weather, the sea is seen hence, and the thread of
smoke from its steamers. The head of Windermere
lies like a pond below : the little Blelham tarn, near
Wray Castle, glitters behind ; and range beyond range
of hills recedes to the horizon. Near at hand, all is

very wild. The Ambleside road winds up steeply between grey rocks and moorland pasture, and dashing streams; and the Kirkstone mountain has probably mists driving about its head. There is something wilder to come, however, — the noted Kirkstone Pass, — the great pass of the district. The descent begins about a quarter of a mile beyond the house. Down plunges the road, with rock and torrent on either hand, and the bold sweeps of Coldfield and Scandale Screes shutting in the pass; and the little lake of Brothers' Water lying below, afar off among the green levels; and, closing in the whole in front, the mass of Place Fell, — the other side of which goes sheer down into Ullswater. The stranger must not omit to observe near the head of the pass, the fallen rock, ridged like a roof, whose form (like that of a miniature church) has given its name to its precincts. All the way as he descends to Brothers' Water, the openings on the Scandale side (the left) charm his eye, — with their fissures, precipices, green slopes and levels, and knolls in the midst, crowned with firs. He passes through Hartsop, and then winds on, for three or four miles, among the rich levels of Patterdale, which is guarded by mountains jutting forwards, like promontories. The Patterdale Inn, kept by Mr. Gelderd, is another of the first-rate hotels of the district. The stranger, who must have left Windermere early in the morning, hastens to order a car or a boat, to take him to Gowbarrow Park, and desires that dinner may await him in about three hours' time.

If the weather is calm and fine, he has a boat, to which he must walk across the meadows. As soon as

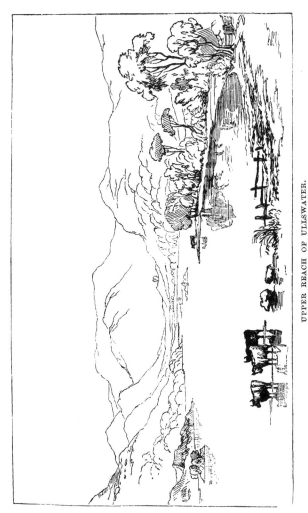

UPPER REACH OF ULLSWATER.

he is afloat, the beauties of Ullswater open upon him,
— the great Place Fell occupying the whole space to
the right; and Stybarrow Crag, precipitous and wooded,
shoots up on the left-hand bank. The road winds
below it, under trees, passing good houses, and the
paths to Helvellyn, and to the lead-works, and to Glen-
coin, — all recesses full of beauty. Ullswater has two
bends, and is shaped like a relaxed Z. At the first
bend, the boat draws to shore, below Lyulph's Tower,
an ivy-covered little castle, built for a shooting-box by
the late Duke of Norfolk; but it stands on the site of
a real old tower, named, it is said, after the Ulf, or
L'Ulf, the first baron of Greystoke, who gave its name
to the lake. Some, however, insist that the real name
is Wolf's Tower. The park which surrounds it, and
stretches down to the lake, is studded with ancient
trees; and the sides of its watercourses, and the depths
of its ravines, are luxuriantly wooded. Vast hills, with
climbing tracks, rise behind, on which the herds of deer
are occasionally seen, like brown shadows from the
clouds. They are safe there from being startled (as they
are in the glades of the park) by strangers who come to
find out Ara Force by following the sound of the fall.
Our tourist must take a guide to this waterfall from
the tower.

He will be led over the open grass to the ravine, and
then along its wooded sides on a pathway above the
brawling stream, till he comes to a bridge, which will
bring him in full view of the fall. As he sits in the
cool damp nook at the bottom of the chasm, where
the echo of dashing and gurgling water never dies, and

the ferns, long grasses and ash sprays wave and quiver everlastingly in the pulsing air; and as, looking up, he sees the slender line of bridge spanning the upper fall, he ought to know of the mournful legend which belongs to this place, and which Wordsworth has preserved: — In the olden times, a knight who loved a lady, and courted her in her father's tower here, at Greystoke, went forth to win glory. He won great glory: and at first his lady rejoiced fully in it: but he was so long in returning, and she heard so much of his deeds in behalf of distressed ladies, that doubts at length stole upon her heart as to whether he still loved her. These doubts disturbed her mind in sleep: and she began to walk in her dreams, directing her steps towards the waterfall where she and her lover used to meet. Under a holly tree beside the fall they had plighted their vows, and this was the limit of her dreaming walks. The knight at length returned to claim her. Arriving in the night, he went to the ravine to rest under the holly until the morning should permit him to knock at the gate of the tower: but he saw a gliding white figure among the trees: and this figure reached the holly before him, and plucked twigs from the tree, and threw them into the stream. Was it the ghost of his lady love? or was it herself? She stood in a dangerous place: he put out his hand to uphold her: the touch awakened her. In her terror and confusion she fell from his grasp into the torrent, and was carried down the ravine. He followed and rescued her; but she died upon the bank; not, however, without having fully understood that her lover was true, and had come to claim her. The knight devoted the rest of his days to mourn her : he built himself a cell upon the spot, and became a hermit for her sake.

The visitor should ascend the steps and pathway from the bottom of the fall, and stand on the bridge that spans the leap. It is a grand thing to look down. He returns the way he came, now by boat, and, after dinner up Kirkstone Pass. He will hear and see enough to make him wish to come again, and stay awhile on Ullswater. He would like to walk along Place Fell, above the margin of the lake, where no carriage road is or can be made ; and, once there, he would certainly climb the mountain. He would like to enter the bridle road, from the other shore, which leads to Grisedale tarn, and comes out above Grasmere. He would like to visit Angle Tarn, on the southern end of Place Fell ; and, yet more, Hays Water, the large lonely tarn above Hartsop ; where the angler delights to seclude himself, because the trout delights in it too. It is a high treat to follow up the beck from the road, winding among the farms, and then entering the solitude of the pass, till the source of the stream is found in this tarn, a mile and a half from the main road. The little lake is over-hung by High Street, so that the Roman eagles, as well as the native birds of the rocks, may have cast their shadows upon its surface. Its rushy and rocky margin is as wild a place as the most adventurous angler can ever have found himself in. Our traveller must, how-ever, come again to see it ; for there is no time to diverge to it to-day.

At the house, at the top of the pass, (which he has

walked up, in mercy to his horses) he leaves the Troutbeck road to the left, and descends rapidly upon
Ambleside, which is between three and four miles from
the house. On the left, is the valley or ravine of the
Stock, whose waters are concealed by wood. The road
runs along the slopes of the Scandale Fells. Below,
Windermere opens more and more; and at length, the
pretty little town of Ambleside appears, nestling at the
foot of Wansfell, and the valley of the Rotha opens at
the gazer's feet. On the opposite margin of this green
recess, and on the skirts of Loughrigg, he sees Fox
How, the residence and favourite retirement of the late
Dr. Arnold, and now inhabited by his family. Near
the pass which opens between Loughrigg and Fairfield,
he is told that the residence of Wordsworth may be
seen from below. Just under him to the left is the old
church; and near the centre of the valley is the new
church, — more of a blemish than an adornment, un-
happily, from its size and clumsiness, and the bad taste
of its architecture. Though placed in a valley, it has
a spire, — the appropriate form of churches in a level
country; and the spire is of a different colour from the
rest of the building; and the east window is remarkably
ugly. There have been various reductions of the beauty
of the valley within twenty years or so; and this latest
is the worst, because the most conspicuous. The old
church, though not beautiful, is suitable to the position,
and venerable by its ancient aspect. It is abundantly
large enough for the place, except for a few weeks in
summer: but its burial ground, inclosed by roads on
three sides, has for many years been overcrowded. Ten

years ago, the state of the churchyard, and the health
of the people who lived near it, was such as to make
the opening of a new burial-ground a pressing matter;
and hence, no doubt, arose the new church, though a
larger and more beautiful cemetery might easily have
been formed in the neighbourhood.

The descent to all the Ambleside inns is steep, —
past the old church, and through a narrow street, and
into the space dignified with the name of the market-
place, and actually exhibiting an ancient market-cross.
Half-a-dozen of the few shops of the town are in or
about the market-place, and the Salutation and Commercial Inns and the White Lion,— the three principal
inns, are all conspicuous in it. If there happens to be
a moon to go home by, the stranger may use the sunset
or twilight hour for seeing Stockghyll Force, while his
horses are refreshing for the remaining five miles. He
is directed or guided through the stable-yard of the
Salutation Inn, when he passes under a tall grove of
old trees on the right hand, and the stream on the left.
On the opposite bank is the bobbin mill, the one in-
dustrial establishment of Ambleside, placed there on
account of the abundant supply of coppice wood obtain-
able in the neighbourhood. The stacks of wood are
seen, high up on the bank; and the ivy-clad dwelling
of the proprietor; and then the great water-wheel,
with its attendant spouts and weir, and sound of gushing and falling waters. Where the path forks towards
and away from the stream, the visitor must take the
left-hand one. The other is the way up Wansfell. His
path leads him under trees, and up and up through a

charming wood, with the water dashing and brawling
further and further below, till his ear catches the sound
of the fall: and presently after, the track turns to the
left, and brings him to a rocky station whence he has a
full view of the force. It is the fashion to speak lightly
of this waterfall, — it being within half a mile of the
inn, and so easily reached; but it is, in our opinion, a
very remarkable fall, (from the symmetry of its parts,)
and one of the most graceful that can be seen. Its leap,
of about seventy feet, is split by a rocky protrusion,
and intercepted by a ledge running across; so that there
are four falls, — two smaller ones above, answering pre-
cisely to each other, and two larger leaps below, no less
exactly resembling. The rock which parts them is
feathered with foliage; and so are the sides of the
ravine. Below, the waters unite in a rocky basin,
whence they flow down to the mill, and on, in a most
picturesque torrent, through a part of Ambleside, and
into the meadows, where they make their last spring
down a rock near Millar Bridge, and join the Rothay
about a mile from the lake.

The remaining five miles are mailroad; so the tourist is within an hour of his inn, — making allowance
for hills, as it is necessary to do in this region. If it
is light enough, he will see how beautifully the Brathay
valley, graced with its pretty church, opens to the
right. He will not pass by the field at Waterhead,
where remains of a Roman encampment exist: but his
driver can point out the spot. By the time he reaches
the tollbar, the scenery will be familiar to him; —
Clappersgate along the head of the lake; and the pier

where the steamers stop; and then Wray Castle on the opposite shore; and, on his left-hand, Wansfell Holme, and the gate to Dove's Nest; and then, Lowwood Inn; and soon after, Ecclerigg; and then Calgarth, Bishop Watson's house, now inhabited by Edward Swinburne, Esq.; then, on the left, Ibbotsholme, the residence of Samuel Taylor, Esq.: and, over Troutbeck bridge (the outlet of the stream he first skirted in the morning), and on to Cook's House, and up the last steep ascent to Windermere. His landlord has a hospitable welcome for him, at his comfortable hotel; and he has earned his good meal and night's rest by an arduous day's work. Every stage of it, however, has been full of delights.

THIRD TOUR.

BY THE FERRY, AND THE WRAY, AND BRATHAY VALLEY, TO
HIGH CLOSE, AND DOWN RED BANK TO GRASMERE AND
EASEDALE, AND THENCE BY RYDAL TO AMBLESIDE.

The stranger had better take an entire day for this
tour also, if he can spare the time, and means to see
Easedale at his ease. The distance in miles is not a
day's journey; but there are things to see which
deserve a pause.

First, the car must cross to the Ferry House; and
then the road lies along the shore of the lake. In our
opinion, this is the most beautiful portion of the whole
thirty miles of circuit. The road ascends and descends
under the wooded bank, traverses fields and meadows
and little white beaches; passing promontories, coves,
boat-houses and little piers, and obtaining fine views
of the opposite shore, and the Troutbeck hills behind.
After three or four miles of this, the road turns somewhat inland, and passes the entrance-gates of Wray
Castle. The view in the rear of the castle is very wild
and dreary. There is much draining going on; and
this affords promise of future cultivation: but at
present the nearer landscape is made up of wet moorland, with fir plantations on the slopes; and Blelham
Tarn lying cold and unlovely in the midst. Soon, however, Pullwyke Bay comes into view, with the well-

drained meadows around it, and Pull Cottage, on its terrace, with sloping gardens, overlooking the inlet. A large house, surrounded by spacious gardens, is in course of erection on a fine slope, with a southern aspect, near Major Rogers's cottage. The road is cut out of the rock, or bordered with wood, from Pullwyke till the little Brathay Church comes into view,— stationed on its wooded knoll, and backed by Loughrigg. At this point the Langdale Pikes, and other fine peaks come into view to the left, while the quiet Brathay valley opens in front. If the stranger has any thought of going up Loughrigg, some other day, he may now see the path by which he may ascend or descend ; — a zigzag path, mounting from Clappersgate, and leading up to the two peaks, crowning the south end of Loughrigg, from between which the most perfect possible view of Windermere is obtained. That cannot be done to-day ; but the traveller will not forget that that must be his way up or down.

He has now to turn to the left, on reaching the valley ; and when he sees the churchyard gate, he must alight, and walk up to the church. From the rock there he commands the mountain range from Coniston Old Man to the Langdale Pikes : the Brathay flows beneath, through its quiet meadows ; and its dashing among the rocks, just under his feet, catches his ear ; — Loughrigg, with its copses and crags and purple heather, rises immediately before him : and to the right he sees a part of Ambleside nestling between the hills, and a stretch of the lake. This churchyard has the first daffodils and snowdrops on the southern side of its rock ;

and, in its copse, the earliest wood anemones. Throughout the valley, spring flowers, and the yellow and
white broom abound.

The road ascends and descends abruptly, and winds
towards, and away from, the right bank of the Brathay,
till it reaches Skelwith Fold. There the stranger must
alight again, and go through a field gate to the right,
to a rocky point, where he commands the finest view
of the valley and its environs. And again, just before
he comes to Skelwith Bridge, he must go through the
gap in the wall to the left, and follow the field-track
until he comes in sight of Skelwith Force. He will
hardly aver that he ever saw a more perfect picture
than this, — with the fall in the centre, closed in by
rock and wood on either hand, and by the Langdale
Pikes behind. Returning to his car, he will next pass
over the bridge, and the roaring torrent beneath, and
by stacks of wood, — (more coppice wood for another
bobbin mill,) and, turning to the right, will find that
he has headed the valley. As he is not going home,
however, but to Grasmere, he turns out of the Brathay
valley by a steep road on the left, which ascends again
and again, leading by farmsteads almost as primitive as
those of Troutbeck, and evidently mounting the spurs,
of Loughrigg, — which he is travelling round to-day,
and which must therefore be always on his right hand.
After a while, he comes to a sheet of water, so still, if
the day be calm, that he might possibly miss it, unless
the precision of the reflections should strike his eye.
It is more likely, however, to be rippled by some
breeze, and to show how deeply blue, or darkly grey,

these mountain tarns may be. This is Loughrigg tarn, well known to all readers of Wordsworth. At some little distance beyond it, the stranger must diverge from his road, to visit High Close, and see the view which is reputed the finest in Westmorland. He may leave his car where the road to High Close ascends to the left, and walk to the farm house at the top. As there are probably lodgers, he had better not present himself at the garden door, but go on to the farmyard gate, pass through the yard to the field, and walk along the brow till he reaches the grey stone bench. There he is! overlooking "the finest view in Westmorland." To the extreme right, Bowfell closes in the Langdale valley, the head of which is ennobled by the swelling masses of the Pikes. A dark cleft in the nearer one is the place where the celebrated Dungeon Ghyll Force is plunging and foaming, beyond the reach of eye and ear. He can gather from this station, something of the character of Langdale. It has levels, here expanding, there contracting; and the stream winds among them from end to end. There is no lake : and the mountains send out spurs, alternating or meeting, so as to make the levels sometimes circular and sometimes winding. The dwellings are on the rising grounds which skirt the levels ; and this, together with the paving of the road below, shows that the valley is subject to floods. The houses, of grey stone, each on its knoll, with a canopy of firs and sycamores above it, and ferns scattered all around, and ewes and lambs nestling near it, — these primitive farms are cheerful and pleasant objects to look upon, whether

from above or passing among them. Nearer at hand
are some vast quarries of blue slate. Below, among
plantations, are seen the roofs of the Elterwater Powder
Mills; whence the road winds through the village of
Langdale Chapel, to the margin of the pools which
make up the lake. From their opposite shore rise the
hills, height above height, — range beyond range. To
the left lies Loughrigg Tarn, and, in the distance,
Windermere, with Wray Castle prominent on its
height, and the Lancashire hills closing in the view.
It is a singular prospect, at once noble and lovely;
and the comfortable lodgings at High Close farm are
in request accordingly.

The car is waiting where the traveller left it ; but he
had better walk for half a mile or so, — the descent of
Red Bank being very steep. The great mountain that
swells so grandly above the rest before him is Helvellyn.
The lake that opens below is Grasmere, with its one
island, made up of green slope, black fir clump, and
grey barn. At the further end lies the village, with its
old square church tower, beneath whose shadow Wordsworth is buried. The white road that winds like a
ribbon up and up the gap between Helvellyn and the
opposite fells is the mail road to Keswick, and the gap
is Dunmail Raise. The remarkable and beautiful hill
behind the village is Helm Crag ; and its rocky crest
forms the group called the Lion and the Lamb. The
long white house, near the foot of Helvellyn, is the
Swan Inn, whence Scott, Southey, and Wordsworth,
set forth on ponies for the ascent of the mountain : and
behind it rises the path by which pedestrians come from

GRASMERE, FROM RED BANK.

Grasmere to Patterdale, by the margin of Grisedale
tarn, — the mountain tarn of the wild boar, as the
words properly signify. To the left of Helm Crag, a
deep valley evidently opens. That is Easedale; and
there our tourist is to go to-day. Meantime, let him
linger awhile, that he may learn by heart every feature
of this gay and lovely scene. The lane he has just
passed to the right leads him to the grassy road called
Loughrigg terrace, whence the best views are obtained
of both Grasmere and Rydal lakes, and which leads
along the uplands and then by Rydal Lake back to the
valley of the Rothay. We must leave it now, and
plunge down Red Bank, which has the characteristics of
a Norwegian road. At the cistern at the bottom, the
stranger enters his car, and passes farm houses between
him and the lake, and villas on the rocky and wooded
bank on the left; and, at the corner, where the road
turns to the village, the cluster of lodging-houses,
called St. Oswald's, where the Hydropathic Establishment struggled on for a time, but found the Westmorland winters too long for invalids.

The driver must stop at the Red Lion, to order
dinner. It is an old-fashioned little place, where the
traveller's choice is usually between ham and eggs and
eggs and ham; with the addition, however, of cheese
and oat cake. He goes to the Red Lion now merely
because it is on the way to his destination. If he were
going to stay at Grasmere, he would take up his abode
at the Hollins and Lowther Hotel, kept by Mr. Brown.
The beauty of the view from that house is evident at a
glance; and good accommodations will be found within,

with ample means of conveyance of all kinds. What-
ever the dinner at the Red Lion is to be, it must
not be ready under two or three hours ; — rather three
than two. He proceeds for a mile between fences before
he reaches the opening of Easedale. The gate and
shrubbery to the right are the entrance to Lady
Richardson's cottage ; and there the regular road ends.
The car can go about a mile further along the farm
tracks in the valley, through the meadows which yield
a coarse hay, and near the stream which is tufted with
alders. At the farm house where the car stops, the
people will shew the stranger the way he must go, —
past the plantation, and up the hill side where he will
find the track that will guide him up to the waterfall,
— the foaming cataract which is seen all over the valley,
and is called Sour Milk Ghyll Force. The water and
the track together will show him the way to the tarn,
which is the source of the stream. Up and on he goes,
over rock and through wet moss, with long stretches of
dry turf and purple heather ; and at last, when he is
heated and breathless, the dark cool recess opens, in
which lies Easedale Tarn. Perhaps there is an angler
standing beside the great boulder on the brink. Perhaps there is a shepherd lying among the ferns. But
more probably the stranger finds himself perfectly alone.
There is perhaps nothing in natural scenery which
conveys such an impression of stillness as tarns which
lie under precipices : and here the rocks sweep down to
the brink almost round the entire margin. For hours
together the deep shadows move only like the gnomon
of the sundial ; and, when movement occurs, it is not

such as disturbs the sense of repose; — the dimple
made by a restless fish or fly, or the gentle flow of
water in or out; or the wild drake and his brood, pad-
dling so quietly as not to break up the mirror, or the
reflection of some touch of sunlight, or passing shadow.
If there is commotion from gusts or eddies of wind,
the effect is even more remarkable. Little white clouds
are driven against the rocks, — the spray is spilled in
unexpected places; now the precipices are wholly veiled,
and there is nothing but the ruffled water to be seen :
and again, in an instant, the rocks are disclosed so fear-
fully that they seem to be crowding together to crush
the intruder. If this seems to the inexperienced like
extravagance, let him go alone to Easedale Tarn, or to
Angle Tarn on Bowfell, on a gusty day, and see what he
will find.

After his return to the Red Lion, and his dinner, the
stranger will go to the churchyard. In the church is
a medallion portrait of Wordsworth, accompanied by
an inscription adapted from a dedication of Mr. Keble's.
The simple and modest tombstone in the churchyard
will please him better. At present it bears only the
name of the poet, — in his case, an all-sufficient memo-
rial : but it is understood that some dates and other
particulars will be filled in hereafter. Beside him lies
his only daughter, and next to her, her husband, —
whose first wife is next him on the other side. Some
other children of Wordsworth, who died young, are
buried near; and one grandchild. Close behind the
family group lies Hartley Coleridge, at whose funeral
the white-haired Wordsworth attended, not very long

before his own death. This spot, under the yews,
besides the gushing Rothay and encircled by green
mountains, is a fitting resting-place for the poet of the
region. He chose it himself; and every one rejoices
that he did.

Just after entering the mail road, the driver will
point out the cottage in which the poet and his sister
lived, many long years ago, when Scott was their guest.
Several good houses have sprung up near it, within a
few years. The promontory which here causes the lake
to contract to the little river (which is called the Rothay
in all the intervals of the chain of lakes,) may be passed
in three ways. The mail road runs round its point,
and therefore keeps beside the water; — the Roman
road, where the Wishing Gate used to be, crosses it by
a rather steep ascent and descent; — and a shorter road
still, steeper and boggy, cuts across its narrowest part,
and comes out at the Rydal Quarries. Our traveller
will take the mail road, probably. It will soon bring
him to Rydal Lake; and he cannot but think the valley
very lovely in the summer afternoon. On the opposite
side of the lake is Loughrigg, with its terrace-walk
distinctly visible half way up. The islands are wooded;
and on one of them is a heronry; and the grey bird,
with its long flapping wings, is most likely visible,
either in flight, or perched on a tree near its nest, or
fishing in the shallows. Nab Scar, the blunt end of
Fairfield, which overlooks the road and the lake, is very
fine with its water-worn channels, its wood, and grey
rocks. Nab Cottage, the humble white house by the road
side, and on the margin of the lake, is the place where

Hartley Coleridge lived and died. In the distance Ivy Cottage peeps out of the green; and further on, Rydal Chapel rises out of the foliage on the verge of the park.

When the turn to the left, which leads up to that chapel, is reached, the stranger must alight, and ascend it. He is ascending Rydal Mount: and Wordsworth's house is at the top of the hill, — within the modest gate on the left. If the family should be absent, the traveller may possibly obtain entrance, and stand on the mossgrown eminence, (like a little Roman camp,) in front of the house, whence he may view the whole valley of the Rothay to the utmost advantage. Windermere in the distance is, as Wordsworth used to say, a light thrown into the picture, in the winter season, and, in summer, a beautiful feature, changing with every hue of the sky. The whole garden is a true poet's garden; its green hollows, its straight terraces, bordered with beds of periwinkle, and tall foxgloves, purple and white, — (the white being the poet's favourite); and then the summer-house, — (now, however, damp and dreary, with the fircones that line it dropping out of their places); and then the opening of the door, which discloses the other angle of the prospect, — Rydal Pass, with the lake lying below. Every resident in the neighbourhood thinks the situation of his own house the best. We should say that Wordsworth's came next to Mr. Sheldon's at Miller Brow, but for the great disadvantage of the long and steep ascent to it. That ascent is a serious last stage of a walk on a hot summer day; but the privileges of the spot, when once reached, are almost incomparable.

The guide to the Rydal Falls will by this time have presented herself, and the tourist must visit them. They are within the park, and cannot be seen without a guide: but some one is always to be found at one of the two guides' cottages on the ascent of the hill. The upper fall is the finest, in the eyes of those who prefer the most natural accessaries of a cascade: but the lower is the one generally represented by artists, — the summer-house from which it is viewed affording an admirable picture-frame, and the basin of rock, and the bridge above, constituting, in truth, a very perfect picture. When there is a dash of sunshine on the verdure, behind and under the bridge, to contrast with the shadowy basin and pool of the fall, the subject is tempting enough to the artist.

These falls seen, the tourist need alight from his car no more, for he is only a mile and a half from Ambleside, and within seven of his inn. He presently passes Pelter Bridge, which spans the Rothay on the right. That is the way to Fox How: and he presently sees Fox How, — the grey house embosomed in trees, — at the foot of Loughrigg. He must not mistake for it the gem of a house that he sees, — the cream-coloured one, veiled in roses, with the conservatories beside it, just under the wooded precipice: — that is Fox Ghyll, the residence of Hornby Roughsedge, Esq. To the left, there are good views of Rydal Park. Approaching Ambleside, the first house to the left is Lesketh How, the residence of Dr. Davy: the white house to the left is Tranby Lodge, the abode of Alfred Barkworth, Esq.: and the house on the rising ground behind the

chapel is the Knoll, the residence of Miss H. Martineau.
The gates on the left are those of Green Bank, the
estate of Benson Harrison, Esq.; and the pretty cottage
next reached on the same side is that of Miss Head,
called Low Nook. The stream to the right is the
Stock, making its way to the river; and the odd little
grey dwelling built above it is the ancient house which
is considered the most curious relic in Ambleside of the
olden time. The view of the mill and the rocky channel of the Stock on the left of the bridge is the one
which every artist sketches as he passes by; and if there
is in the Exhibition in London, in any year, a View at
Ambleside, it is probably this. The Kirkstone road
now joins the mail road, and the tourist finds himself
on old ground, — in Ambleside market-place.

A DAY ON THE MOUNTAINS.

The stranger has now made his three tours. There is one thing more he must do before he goes on into Cumberland. He must spend a day on the Mountains: and if alone, so much the better. If he knows what it is to spend a day so far above the every-day world, he is aware that it is good to be alone, (unless there is danger in the case); and, if he is a novice, let him try whether it be not so. Let him go forth early, with a stout stick in his hand, provision for the day in his knapsack or his pocket; and, if he chooses, a book: but we do not think he will read to-day. A map is essential, to explain to him what he sees: and it is very well to have a pocket compass, in case of sudden fog, or any awkward doubt about the way. In case of an ascent of a formidable mountain, like Scawfell or Helvellyn, it is rash to go without a guide: but our tourist shall undertake something more moderate, and reasonably safe, for a beginning.

What mountain shall it be? He might go up Blackcombe, on his way to or from Furness: and from thence he might see, in fair weather, as Wordsworth tells us, "a more extensive view than from any other point in Britain," — seven English counties, and seven Scotch, a good deal of Wales, the Isle of Man, and in some lucky moment, just before sunrise (as the Ordnance surveyors say) the coast of Ireland. This is very fine; but it is hardly what is looked for in the lake district, — the sea being the main feature. He might go up the Old Man from Coniston; but there are the copper works, and there is the necessity of a guide: and it is a long way to go for the day's treat. If he ascends the Langdale Pikes, it had better be from some interior station; and the rest of the great peaks will be best commanded from Keswick. Of those within reach of Windermere, which shall it be? Loughrigg is very easy and very charming; but it is not commanding enough. From the surrounding heights it looks like a mere rambling hill. Wansfell is nearest, and also easy and safe. It may be reached by a charming walk from Low Wood Inn, and descended by the Stockghyll lane, above Ambleside. The immediate neighbourhood is mapped out below; and there is a long and wide opening to the south: but to the north-east, and everywhere round the head of the lake, the view is stopped, first by Nab Scar, and then by other heights. Why should it not be Nab Scar itself? or, the whole of Fairfield? That excursion is safe, not over fatiguing, practicable for a summer day, and presenting scenery as characteristic as can be found. Let it be Fairfield.

The stranger had better come on to Ambleside by the early mail, and breakfast there. He must then set off up the road to the Nook, which anybody will show him. The Nook is a farmhouse, in a glorious situation, as he will see when he gets there, and steps

D

into the field on the left, to look abroad from the brow.
He then passes under its old trees to where the voice
of falling waters calls him onward. Scandale Beck
comes tumbling down its rocky channel, close at hand.
He must cross the bridge, and follow the cart road,
which brings him out at once upon the fells. What
he has to aim at is the ridge above Rydal forest or
park, from whence his way is plain, — round the whole
cul-de-sac of Fairfield, to Nab Scar. He sees it all;
and the only thing is to do it: and we know of no
obstacle to his doing it, unless it be the stone wall
which divides the Scandale from the Rydal side of the
ridge. These stone walls are an inconvenience to
pedestrians, and a great blemish in the eyes of
strangers. In the first place, however, it is to be said
that an open way is almost invariably left, up every
mountain, if the rover can but find it; and, in the next
place, the ugliness of these climbing fences disappears
marvellously when the stranger learns how they came
there. — In the old times, when there were wolves, and
when the abbots of the surrounding Norman monas-
teries encouraged their tenants to approach nearer and
nearer to the Saxon fastnesses, the shepherds were
allowed to inclose crofts about their hillside huts, for
the sake of browsing their flocks on the sprouts of the
ash and holly with which the hillsides were then
wooded, and of protecting the sheep from the wolves
which haunted the thickets. The inclosures certainly
spread up the mountain sides, at this day, to a height
where they would not be seen if ancient custom had not
drawn the lines which are thus preserved; and it

appears, from historical testimony, that these fences
existed before the fertile valleys were portioned out
among many holders.   Higher and higher ran these
stone inclosures, — threading the woods, and joining on
upon the rocks.   Now, the woods are for the most part
gone; and the walls offend and perplex the stranger's
eye and mind by their unsightliness and apparent use-
lessness; but it is a question whether, their origin once
known, they would be willingly parted with, — remind-
ing us as they do of the times when the tenants of the
abbots or military nobles formed a link between the
new race of inhabitants and the Saxon remnant of the
old.   One of these walls it is which runs along the
ridge and bounds Rydal Park.   There may be a gate
in it; or one which enables the stranger to get round
it.   If not, he must get over it; and, if he does so
high enough up, it may save him another climb.   The
nearer the ridge, the fewer the remaining walls between
him and liberty.   Once in the forest, Christopher
North's advice comes into his mind, — unspoiled by
the fear, only too reasonable in the lower part of the
park, — of being turned out of the paradise, very sum-
marily.   "The sylvan, or rather, the forest scenery of
Rydal Park," says Professor Wilson, "was, in the
memory of living man, magnificent; and it still contains a treasure of old trees.   By all means wander
away into these old woods, and lose yourself for an
hour or two among the cooing of cushats and the shrill
shriek of startled blackbirds, and the rustle of the
harmless glow-worm among the last year's beech
leaves.   No very great harm should you even fall

asleep under the shadow of an oak, whilst the magpie
chatters at safe distance, and the more innocent squir-
rel peeps down upon you from a bough of the canopy,
and then, hoisting his tail, glides into the obscurity of
the loftiest umbrage." — Ascending from these shades
through a more straggling woodland, the stranger
arrives at a clump on the ridge, — the last clump, and
thenceforth feels himself wholly free. His foot is on
the springy mountain moss; and many a cushion of
heather tempts him to sit down and look abroad.
There may still be a frightened cow or two, wheeling
away, with tail aloft, as he comes onwards; and a few
sheep are still crouching in the shadows of the rocks,
or staring at him from the knolls. If he plays the
child and bleats, he will soon see how many there are.
It is one of the amusements of a good mimic in such
places to bring about him all the animals there are, by
imitating their cries. One may assemble a flock of
sheep, and lead them far out of bounds in this way;
and bewildered enough they look when the bleat ceases,
and they are left to find their way back again. It is
in such places as this that the truth of some of Wordsworth's touches may be recognised, which are most
amusing to cockney readers. Perhaps no passage has
been more ridiculed than that which tells of the
"solemn bleat" of

> "a lamb left somewhere to itself,
> The plaintive spirit of the solitude."

The laughers are thinking of a cattle-market, or a
flock of sheep on a dusty road; and they know nothing
of the effect of a single bleat of a stray lamb high up

on the mountains. If they had ever felt the profound
stillness of the higher fells, or heard it broken by the
plaintive cry, repeated and not answered, they would
be aware that there is a true solemnity in the sound.

Still further on, when the sheep are all left behind,
he may see a hawk perched upon a great boulder. He
will see it take flight when he comes near, and cleave
the air below him, and hang above the woods, — to the
infinite terror, as he knows, of many a small creature
there, and then whirl away to some distant part of the
park. Perhaps a heavy buzzard may rise, flapping,
from its nest on the moor, or pounce from a crag in
the direction of any water-birds that may be about the
springs and pools in the hills. There is no other sound,
unless it be the hum of the gnats in the hot sunshine.
There is an aged man in the district, however, who
hears more than this, and sees more than people below
would, perhaps, imagine. An old shepherd has the
charge of four rain guages which are set up on four
ridges, — desolate, misty spots, sometimes below and
often above the clouds. He visits each once a month,
and notes down what these guages record; and when
the tall old man, with his staff, passes out of sight into
the cloud, or among the cresting rocks, it is a striking
thought that science has set up a tabernacle in these
wildernesses, and found a priest among the shepherds.
That old man has seen and heard wonderful things : —
has trod upon rainbows, and been waited upon by a
dim retinue of spectral mists. He has seen the hail
and the lightnings go forth as from under his hand,
and has stood in the sunshine, listening to the thunder

growling, and the tempest bursting beneath his feet.
He well knows the silence of the hills, and all the
solemn ways in which that silence is broken.   The
stranger, however, coming hither on a calm summer
day, may well fancy that a silence like this can never
be broken.

Looking abroad, what does he see?   The first impression probably is of the billowy character of the
mountain groups around and below him.   This is perhaps the most striking feature of such a scene to a
novice; and the next is the flitting character of the
mists.   One ghostly peak after another seems to rise
out of its shroud; and then the shroud winds itself
round another.   Here the mist floats over a valley;
there it reeks out of a chasm : here it rests upon a
green slope ; there it curls up a black precipice.   The
sunny vales below look like a paradise, with their
bright meadows and waters and shadowy woods, and
little knots of villages.   To the south there is the
glittering sea; and the estuaries of the Leven and
Duddon, with their stretches of yellow sands.   To the
east there is a sea of hill tops.   On the north, Ullswater
appears, grey and calm at the foot of black precipices ;
and nearer may be traced the whole pass from Patterdale, where Brothers' Water lies invisible from hence.
The finest point of the whole excursion is about the
middle of the *cul-de-sac*, where, on the northern sides,
there are tremendous precipices, overlooking Deep-
dale, and other sweet recesses far below.   Here, within
hearing of the torrents which tumble from those precipices, the rover should rest.   He will see nothing so

fine as the contrast of this northern view with the long
green slope on the other side, down to the source of
Rydal Beck, and then down and down to Rydal Woods
and Mount.   He is now 2,950 feet above the sea level;
and he has surely earned his meal.   If the wind troubles
him, he can doubtless find a sheltered place under a
rock.   If he can sit on the bare ridge, he is the more
fortunate.

The further he goes, the more amazed he is at the
extent of the walk, which looked such a trifle from
below.   Waking out of a reverie, an hour after dinner,
he sees that the sun is some way down the western
sky.   He hastens on, not heeding the boggy spaces,
and springing along the pathless heather and moss,
seeing more and more lakes and tarns every quarter of
an hour.   In the course of the day he sees ten.   Windermere, and little Blelham Tarn beyond, he saw first.
Ullswater was below him to the north when he dined;
and, presently after, a tempting path guided his eye to
Grisedale Tarn, lying in the pass from Patterdale to
Grasmere.   Here are four.   Next, comes Grasmere,
with Easedale Tarn above it, in its mountain hollow :
then Rydal, of course, at his feet; and Elterwater
beyond the western ridges; and finally, to the south-
west, Esthwaite Water and Coniston.   There are the
ten.   Eight of these may be seen at once from at least
one point — Nab Scar, whence he must take his last
complete survey; for from hence he must plunge down
the steep slope, and bid farewell to all that lies behind
the ridge.   The day has gone like an hour.   The sunshine is leaving the surface of the nearer lakes, and the

purple bloom of the evening is on the further mountains; and the gushes of yellow light between the
western passes show that sunset is near. He must
hasten down, — mindful of the opening between the
fences, which he remarked from below, and which, if
he finds, he cannot lose his way. He does not seriously
lose his way, though crag and bog made him diverge
now and then. Descending between the inclosures,
he sits down once or twice, to relieve the fatigue to the
ancle and instep of so continuous a descent, and to
linger a little over the beauty of the evening scene.
As he comes down into the basin where Rydal Beck
makes its last gambols and leaps, before entering the
park, he is sensible of the approach of night. Loughrigg seems to rise : the hills seem to close him in, and
the twilight to settle down. He comes to a gate, and
finds himself in the civilised world again. He descends
the green lane at the top of Rydal Mount, comes out
just above Wordsworth's gate, finds his car at the
bottom of the hill, — (the driver beginning to specu
late on whether any accident has befallen the gentleman on the hills,) — is driven home, and is amazed, on
getting out, to find how stiff and tired he is. He
would not, however, but have spent such a day for ten
times the fatigue. He will certainly ascend Helvellyn,
and every other mountain that comes in his way.

EXCURSIONS

TO AND FROM

KESWICK.

EXCURSIONS.

Note. — *The asterisks (*) at the beginning of paragraphs denote objects at the left-hand side of the road, and the figures the distance in miles from the starting point.*

FROM THE SWAN INN GRASMERE TO KESWICK.

1¼. * Tollbar. — From this point the road rises in a steep though gradual ascent to an elevation of 720 feet.

1¼. Fairfield and Seat Sandal.

1¼. * Helm Crag. — A singularly-shaped hill, affording from its summit a delightful prospect. The curious appearance presented by its rugged apex has given rise to some fanciful comparisons. Seen from one part of the valley it strikingly resembles a lion couchant, with a lamb lying at its nose: from another, an old woman cowering. Wordsworth in his " Johanna," designates it as

"That ancient woman seated on Helm Crag."

And again, in the " Waggoner," thus alludes to this singular appearance, giving, as will be seen, a companion to the Ancient Woman.

"The Astrologer, sage Sidrophel,
Where at his desk he nightly sits,
Puzzling on high his curious wits;

He, whose domain is held in common,
With no one but the ancient woman :
Cowering beside her rightful cell,
As if intent on magic spell.
Dread pair, that, spite of wind and weather,
Still sit upon Helm Crag together !"

$2\frac{1}{2}$. Dunmail Raise. — This celebrated pass admits
the traveller into Cumberland. A Cairn, or pile of
stones, is said by tradition, to have been raised here, in
the year 945, by Edmund, the Anglo Saxon King,
in commemoration of a victory gained over Dunmail,
the British King of Cumbria. The British King was
slain here, and his territory given to Malcolm, King of
Scotland. Part of this cairn still remains.

" They now have reached that pile of stones
Heap'd over brave King Dunmail's bones :
He who once held supreme command,
Last King of rocky Cumberland ;
His bones, and those of all his power,
Slain here in a disastrous hour." — WORDSWORTH.

$3\frac{1}{2}$. *Horse Head Inn, Wythburn. — Opposite the
inn stands the small chapel described by Wordsworth as

" Wythburn's modest house of prayer,
As lonely as the lowliest dwelling."

The small hamlet is Wythburn village, locally termed
the " city."

$3\frac{1}{2}$. The road passes along the base of the mighty
Helvellyn. The ascent of Helvellyn is very frequently
commenced from the Horse Head Inn : the distance
from this point being shorter than from any other
station ; though the acclivity, it should be mentioned,

is so steep as to render the attempt, as an equestrian feat to be attended with some degree of danger if not provided with a guide and a sure-footed pony.

4¼. *Thirlmere Lake or Wythburn Water, or, as it is sometimes called, Leathes Water. — An irregular area of water measuring in length about two and a half miles, narrowing in its middle part to a channel, over which is thrown a wooden bridge. Some grandly-frowning precipices overhang the eastern side of the lake. Eagle Crag at its upper, and Raven Crag at its lower, or north end, form distinguished features in the scene.

6. King's Head Inn. — At the sixth milestone from Grasmere, a divergence from the main road to the left, will carry the pedestrian over the wooden bridge, crossing to the western shore, rejoining the turnpike near the fourth milestone. To the picturesque scenery of Thirlmere and its adjuncts, full appreciation can only be given by making this *detour*.

7¼. Losing sight of the lake for a time, on descending into the vale of Legberthwaite, a noble view, stretching down the vales of Legberthwaite and St. John's, reveals itself; on the right an extension of the Helvellyn range; and on the left, the rocky fells of Naddle, bound in the scene; whilst Blencathra, with its furrowed front and peculiarly-shaped summit, which has given to it the more modern name of Saddleback, stands out in the distance, forming an admirable back-ground. Green Crag, better known perhaps by its classic name of the "Castle Rock," is situated at the entrance of the valley of St. John, to the right. It is the scene of Sir Walter Scott's charming romance of

the " Bride of Triermain," though its magic halls have
long since melted away, its massive walls and turrets
still remain, for

> " When a pilgrim strays
> In morning mist, or evening maze,
> Along the mountain lone,
> That fairy fortress often mocks
> His gaze upon the castled rocks
> Of the valley of St. John."

7¼. Smaithwaite Bridge.—Crossing St John's beck,
which issues from Thirlmere. Shoulthwaite Moss.
10¾. Summit of Castlerigg.—The descent of Castlerigg hill unfolds without exception, the richest mountain scenery in England.

KESWICK.

Keswick forms a good central station from which the
northern Lakes' District may be conveniently visited.
The Hotels are Royal Oak, Queen's Head, George,
King's Arms, &c. Staple Manufactory, — Blacklead
Pencils and Woollen Goods. The Institutions, Public
Buildings, &c., are Keswick Library, 2,000 volumes ;
Mechanics' Institution, 500 volumes, with newspapers,
periodicals, &c. ; and the Gentlemen's and Tradesmen's
News Room. Population in 1851, 2,618.

The Parish Church of Crosthwaite, distant about
three-quarters of a mile from the town, in a northerly
direction, is an ancient structure, dedicated to St. Ken-
tigern, alias St. Mungo. The interior was restored in
1845, at an expense of £4,500, principally defrayed by

James Stanger, Esq., Lairthwaite. The mortal remains of Robert Southey, late poet laureate, are intered in the churchyard. In the church is placed a full length recumbent figure of the poet, in white marble, from the studio of Lough. Here also is an ancient monument of the Radcliffe family, beneath which repose two full-length figures of a knight and lady. The baptismal font in use, evidently belongs to a remote period, and forms an interesting object of study to the antiquarian.

Crosthwaite's Museum contains a variety of ancient British, Roman, Saxon, and Norman antiquities, found chiefly in Cumberland and Westmorland; numerous specimens of rocks, minerals, plants, &c., illustrating the natural history of the district; Roman and early English coins; both home and foreign curiosities; manuscript and black-letter volumes; also some good specimens of early typography.

Greta Hall, for upwards of forty years the residence of Southey, stands on rising ground about 200 yards to the right of the bridge crossing the Greta, at the northern extremity of the town.

An inspection of the Pencil Mills will well repay a visit.

St. John's Church, situate at the upper end of the town, was erected in 1839 by the late John Marshall, Esq., M.P., Leeds, at a cost of £6,000. Mr. Marshall's remains, as well as those of the Rev. Frederick Myers, the late revered incumbent, repose in the interior. At a short distance is the Parsonage, the residence of the present incumbent, the Rev. T. D. H. Battersby, M.A.

Flintoft's Model is on view daily at the Town Hall,

constructed on a scale of three inches to a mile: measures twelve feet nine inches by nine feet three inches, including the whole of the Lake District, and is beautifully coloured after nature. To the tourist this specimen of geographical modelling is peculiarly interesting. Drs. Buckland, Dalton, Professor Sedgwick, and a host of other scientific men have borne testimony to its perfect accuracy as a work of art.

The Druids Temple, situate one and a half miles from Keswick, a little to the right of the old road leading to Penrith, consists of rough unhewn stones, forty-eight in number, describing a figure approaching in form to an oval : with a rectangular recess on the east side, formed of lesser stones. The site is of commanding elevation, and affords a fine view of mountain scenery : the whole of Skiddaw, Blencathra, and Helvellyn ranges presenting themselves prominently before the eye of the spectator.

Castlehead Rock is within a quarter of a mile of the town, and commands an extensive view of Derwent Lake, vale and surrounding mountains.

Walla Crag is a still more commanding eminence, overlooking the whole valley. To those who do not make the ascent of Skiddaw, a visit to this place is strongly recommended.

CIRCUIT OF DERWENT LAKE FROM KESWICK.

Lake Derwent approaches in form the oval; measuring in length about three miles, from north to south, by one mile in breadth. Lord's Island, formerly the

property of the Earls of Derwentwater, is the largest,
containing an area of about six acres. The castle was
destroyed consequent on the attainder of the last Earl,
in 1,715, and the estates forfieted to the crown, by
whom they were presented to Greenwich Hospital.
The crumbled foundation-walls of this once princely
mansion are all that are now visible. Vicar's Isle is
the summer residence of Henry C. Marshall, Esq., of
Leeds. St. Herbert's Isle is famous as the retreat of
the saint from whom it derives its name. He died in the
year 687. The cell of the recluse is still pointed out.
The other Islets are Rampsholme, two Lingholms,
Tripetholm, and Otter Isle. The royalty of the lake
is held by Reginald D. Marshall, Esq., General Wynd-
ham, Rowland P. Standish, Esq., and the freeholders
of Borrowdale.

2.   *Barrow House, the abode of S. Z. Langton, Esq.,
J.P.   One of the finest cascades in the district is
situate behind this residence; the fall is over two suc-
cessive ledges of rock, in all 124 feet high. By apply-
ing at the lodge, visitors are permitted to pass through
the grounds to the cascade.

3.   * Lowdore Hotel. — Behind the hotel is the
celebrated waterfall of Lowdore, formed by the stream
descending from the valley of Watendlath, and falling
between two gigantic rocks — Gowdar Crag on the left
and Shepherd's Crag on the right. From the top of
the fall, a beautiful view of the lake and vale below will
be enjoyed. The water falls, in a succession of leaps
or bounds, a height of 120 feet.

4.   Village of Grange.

DERWENT WATER FROM CASTLE HEAD.

5. *One mile above Grange, at the foot of the Borrowdale valley, stands, on a high natural platform, Bowder Stone, a huge fragment of rock, evidently displaced from the precipices above, and poised here, on plain ground, upon one of its angles, similar to a ship resting upon its keel. A pleasant glimpse into the interior of Borrowdale is obtained from the summit of this rock. Upon this account it is generally visited by those who do not intend to explore the valley itself. On the opposite side of the river to Bowder Stone, rises Castle Crag, a high rock, almost detached from the surrounding mountains, and said to have been used as a natural fortress, first by the Romans, then the Saxons, and afterwards the Furness Monks, to whom all Borrowdale was given, it is supposed, by one of the Derwentwater family. Relics found there at various periods, strengthen this supposition.

Return to Grange, cross the bridge over the river Derwent, and pass through the village to the western shore of the lake.

5½. Brandilow Lead Mines.

7 Derwentwater Bay. — The residence of Major General Sir John Woodford stands at the head of the bay, embowered in wood.

9. Portinscale and adjacent villas.

FROM KESWICK, BY BORROWDALE, TO BUTTERMERE.

A mile from Bowder Stone, the village of Rosthwaite is reached. The view from here is bounded on all sides by lofty mountains of rugged aspect, among which

E

may be more especially noted, in front, Glaramara,
Scawfell Pikes, Scawfell and Great Gavel. Half a mile
beyond the village, and near to the chapel, a track
strikes off to the left, leading through Stonethwaite
Village ; thence through the wild and cheerless vale of
Langstreth, over the mountain pass known as the
Stake, into the vale of Langdale. The entrance into
Cumberland or Westmorland, by this route, according
as the traveller is proceeding north or south, is frequently preferred by pedestrians, and, when the weather
is suitable, amply repays the bodily fatigue of the
journey, by the majestic solitude of the scenery it
affords. Following the road to the right, we pass into
the vale of Seathwaite, as far as Seatollar, a neat-looking
substantial building, the residence of Abraham Fisher,
Esq., J.P. Here another track strikes off to the left,
leading to Wastwater by Sty Head, passing the celebrated Blacklead Mines. The rock in which this ore
is found is termed, by the most approved geologists, a
grey porphyritic felspar, and, unlike other ore, is found
lying embedded in, what is termed by the workmen,
sops or bellies, rather than in continuous veins. The
mine has now been closed for some time, on account of
the unproductive yield of late years. In this vicinity
stands a remarkable group of yew trees, — four of
larger size, with several others of lesser growth. Of
the former, one which, for its vigour and size, ranks
among the finest specimens in England, measures
twenty-one feet in circumference, at a height of four
feet from the ground. In the " Excursion," Wordsworth thus commemorates these remarkable trees.

After noticing the large yew, the "pride of Lorton vale," he proceeds:

> Worthier still of note
> Are those fraternal four of Borrowdale,
> Joined in one solemn and capacious grove;
> Huge trunks! and each particular trunk a growth
> Of intertwisted fibres serpentine,
> Up-coiling and inveterately convolved, —
> Nor uninform'd with phantasy, and looks
> That threaten the profane : — a pillar'd shade,
> Upon whose grassless floor of red-brown hue,
> By sheddings from the piring umbrage tinged
> Perennially — beneath whose sable roof
> Of boughs, as if for festal purpose, deck'd
> With unrejoicing berries, ghostly shapes
> May meet at noontide — Fear, and trembling Hope,
> Silence, and Foresight — Death the skeleton,
> And Time, the shadow, there to celebrate,
> As in a natural temple, scattered o'er
> With altars undisturb'd of mossy stone,
> United, worship; or, in mute repose,
> To lie and listen to the mountain flood
> Murmuring from Glaramara's inmost caves.

From Seatollar, the Buttermere road ascends over rough and steep ground, by the side of a stream or ghyll, to the summit of the hause or pass, a height of 800 feet above the Lake Derwent, and 1100 feet above the level of the sea. Some beautiful retrospective views of the receding valley of Borrowdale, and the mountains emerging upon the sight, will be enjoyed in the lingering ascent. Helvellyn is seen to the east, rearing his head over the Watendlath mountains.

The descent into the head of the dale of Buttermere

is rapid, passing between Honister Crag, on the left, and Yew Crag on the right, both of which yield, from several quarries, blue roofing slate of the finest quality, and the former of which rises from the dale to an elevation of 1,700 feet. The road crosses and recrosses twice the descending rivulet, until it reaches Gatesgarth, a farm-building placed "under the most extraordinary amphitheatre of mountainous rocks that ever eye beheld," and thence bordering, for some distance, the shore of the lake. Hasness, a sheltered retreat, the residence of General Benson, is passed on the left, shortly after which the hamlet of Buttermere is reached. From the Inn at Buttermere a visit to Scale force is generally made. This is the highest waterfall in the English Lakes' District, the water falling, in one clear bound, from a height of 156 feet, in another, 44 feet.

> " It springs, at once, with sudden leap,
> Down from the immeasurable steep,
> From rock to rock, with shivering .force rebounding."

Buttermere Lake measures in length about 1½ miles, by half a mile in breadth. A stream connects it with Crummock Lake, which last measures about three miles in length, by three-quarters of a mile broad. Both lakes are famed for the quality of their trout and char.

The return to Keswick from Buttermere may be made either by way of Buttermere Hause, through the peaceful vale of Newlands, a distance of nine miles, or by way of Scale Hill, the head of Lorton Vale and Whinlatter. Both routes equally afford a pleasing variety of vale and mountain scenery.

FROM KESWICK TO WASTWATER, BY STY HEAD.

This excursion is usually made with a guide and ponies. The road, as far as Seatollar, has been already described. A conveyance is sometimes taken as far as Seathwaite; beyond this, however, the road becomes a mere mountain track, fit only for ponies accustomed to the work.

12. Sty Head is a magnificent mountain pass, the highest part of which is 1,250 feet above the nearest dwelling-house. Two sheets of water crown its summit — Sty Head Tarn, close by which the road passes, and Sprinkling Tarn, some half a mile further to the east; beyond the former, the bold and lofty crag of Great End rises abruptly on the left, and still further south, the Pikes of Scawfell. Great Gable is seen on the right. From this place a steep winding path descends rapidly to Wasdale Head, a small upland valley, of some few hundred acres, at the head of Wastwater, and inhabited by a few families, chiefly engaged in sheep farming.

20. From the village of Wasdale the road approaches the Lake, along the margin of which it passes to the Strands, where are two small inns, affording refreshment to tourists. Wastwater is about three and a-half miles in length and half a mile broad; it is remarkable for the depth and purity of its waters, which have never been known to freeze over. It is well stocked with trout, and also contains char. The mountains surrounding it are lofty and majestic. The Screes is a loose mass of shivering rock, extending along the whole length of the south-east shore and shelving

E 3

into the water.   The vicinity affords, from different
points, some striking mountain scenes.   From Strands
to Gosforth is a distance of four miles, whence an ad-
ditional three miles brings the tourist to Calder Bridge,
where there are two excellent inns.   Here lodgings are
usually taken for the night.   A pleasant walk of three-
quarters of a mile along the banks of the river Calder
will enable the reader to visit the venerable ruins of
Calder Abbey.   It formerly belonged to the Cistercian
Monks, for whom it was founded A.D. 1,134, by the
second Ranulph des Meschines.

The return to Keswick will be best made by Enner-
dale Bridge, Lamplugh Cross, Loweswater and Scale
Hill, a distance of thirty miles.   During this second
day's journey much pleasing variety of country will be
passed through.

THE CIRCUIT OF BASSENTHWAITE LAKE.

This lake measures four miles in length and, in some
parts, about one mile in breadth.   It lies three miles to
the north of Lake Derwent, with which it is connected
by the River Derwent.   A pleasant drive of eighteen
miles may be made round it.   The approach is generally
prefered by the western shore.   This is made by the
Cockermouth road as far as Peel Wyke, passing through
the pleasant village of Portinscale, the townships of
Braithwaite and Thornthwaite, thence through Wythop
Woods.   The northern end of the lake is rounded by
crossing Ouse Bridge, and proceeding by Armathwaite
Hall, the seat of Sir F. Vane, to Castle Inn.   From

this place the road takes a southerly direction, passing through the rich and fertile vale of Bassenthwaite, thence for some distance along the foot of Skiddaw to Keswick.

ASCENT OF SKIDDAW.

If the weather be at all propitious, no stranger should leave Keswick without making a mountain ascent. Skiddaw is generally prefered, on account of the short distance from the town, and the comparative ease with which the journey may be made, either on foot or in the saddle. At the Penrith tollbar, about half a mile to the east of Keswick, the road crosses the Greta. Opposite Greta Bank, turn to the left, thence wind round Latrigg, to the point where the ascent commences. The path runs parallel with a wall for a considerable distance up the steepest part of the mountain ; afterwards, however, leaving the wall to the right, a direct line forward leads to an almost level tract of moor, from which further progress is of gradual ascent. Half-a-dozen different summits, each marked by a pile of stones, and each presenting varying and peculiar views, are passed before gaining the highest point. The view from this place must be seen to be appreciated, — no description could make it understood. Skiddaw, it should be stated, stands at an elevation of 3,022 feet above the sea level. The distance of its highest point is six miles from Keswick.

FROM KESWICK, BY ULLSWATER, TO PATTERDALE.

The approach to Ullswater may be made from Keswick by several different routes. The pedestrian might take the Ambleside road for about four and three-quarter miles, and then, turning to the left, pursue a foot-path passing over the north shoulder of Helvellyn, making the descent by way of Greenside Lead Mines; or, at the third milestone on the Penrith road, a bridle-road leads, by way of Wanthwaite, to Hilltop and Threlkeld Pasture, to Dockray.

Taking, however, the usual route, a distance of four and a-half miles on the Penrith road brings the traveller to the village of Threlkeld, a little beyond which, to the right, is situated Threlkeld Hall, once the residence of Sir Lancelot Threlkeld, a knight of the reign of Henry VII., but now a somewhat antiquated farmhouse. This Sir Lancelot married the widow of Lord Clifford, who was slain in the civil wars in 1461. Their son, young Clifford, was preserved from the fury of the Yorkist faction, and brought hither out of the way of all search. Twenty-four years of his life were spent here, leading the life of a shepherd. On the union of the houses of York and Lancaster, his estates and honours were restored to him. He attended parliament, when summoned by his sovereign, and served in the war which ended in the victory of Flodden Field, in which he took part; but his life was chiefly passed in the country, restoring his castles, which had gone to decay during the civil war, and following peaceful pursuits.

"Ages after he was laid in earth,
The ' good Lord Clifford ' was the name he bore."

From Threlkeld the road passes along the foot of

Blencathra, as far as the sixth milestone, thence across a moorish tract of country for two or three miles. Ten and a-half miles from Keswick, the road diverges to the right, leaving the turnpike road. A distance of five miles more brings us to Dockray village, a mile and a-half beyond which we reach Lyulph's Tower, in Gowbarrow Park. A beautiful drive of four miles will then bring the traveller to the Inn at Patterdale.

A few days will probably be spent in exploring the district, after which the traveller may either return to Windermere, or reach the railway at Penrith.

ON THE FLOWERING PLANTS, FERNS, AND MOSSES OF WINDERMERE AND ITS NEIGHBOURHOOD.

The banks of Windermere afford many objects of interest to the lover of British wild flowers; so numerous and various, indeed, are the more or less rare plants to be found in the lake itself — in the mountain tarns, streams, woods and bogs, and on the fells and heath, that it is difficult to give a satisfactory account of them in the space of a short chapter. A general description of the Flora of the district may, however, be of some use to the tourist who, in passing through the country, wishes to secure anything which may be worthy of a place in his herbarium or garden. The writer proposes to enumerate the least common plants which have been found within about three miles of the lake, occasionally noticing objects of peculiar interest which are found at a greater distance.

Of the order Ranunculacæe, Thalictrum flavum is not uncommon about the margin of the lake; T. minus is also found. The beautiful globe-flower Trollius europœus is abundant in various situations. Helleborus virdis occurs in two situations near the Windermere terminus, and H. fœtidus grows near the road between Bowness and Kendal: it is very probable that both these are introduced. Aquilegia vulgaris is found in numerous places. — Of the order Nymphœaceœ, Nymphœa alba and Nuphar lutea are frequent in the lake and many of the mountain tarns. Of Papaveraceæ Meconopsis cambrica is not uncommon, and in some places, such as near the Ferry Inn and other parts of Furness Fells, and in Troutbeck it is abundant. Chelidonium majus is common. — Of Fumariaceœ Corydalis, claviculata is not uncommon in healthy places. — Of Cruciferœ, Lepidium Smithii is abundant; L. Draba grows near Newby Bridge. Arabis hirsutes is found on Whitbarrow; Cochlearia officinalis on Kirkstone. — Helianthemum canum, of the order Cistaceæ occurs in Witherslack. — Of Droseraceæ, Drosera rotundifolia is abundant, and D. longifolia is rare.—Of Caryophyllaceæ, Stellaria nemorum is found in some wet woods and ghylls. — Of Malvaceæ Malva moschata is frequent in various places. Of Hypericaceæ, Hypericum androsœmum is not uncommon on wooded fellsides, generally near rivulets. H. quadrangulum and humifusum are common, and H. hirsutum is plentiful on Whitbarrow. — Of Geraniaieæ, Geranium sylvatium is not uncommon ; G. lucidum is frequent; G. sanguineum and pratense are abundant on Whitbarrow. — Of Balsaminaceæ, Impatiens noli me tangere is plentiful on Furness Fells, near the Ferry Inn, at Millerground, Gill Head, and many other places. — Of Leguminifereæ, Genista tinctoria is very abundant and beautiful in heathy places. — Of Rosaceæ, Prunus padus is common. Spiræa salicifolia grows near the Ferry Inn, but this is doubtless introduced, as this plant is now found to be nowhere indigenous in Great Britain. Rubus suberectus

is found in woods and sometimes on open mountain
sides. R. saxatilis occurs in a few places. R. idœus
rhamnifolius, leucostachys and rudis are the most common species of Rubus here. R. chamæmorus grows in
Long Sleddale. We have seen Rosa spinosissima in
one place only. R. villosa is very common. — Of
Haloragiaceæ, Myriophyllum spicatum and verticilla-
tum abound in the lake. — Of Grossulariaceæ, Ribes
rubrum and grossulara are plentiful in the woods. —
Of Crassulaceæ, Sedum telephium and anglicum are
very common; and Cotyledon umbilicus is found in
many places. — Of Saxifragaceæ, Saxifraga aizoides
stellaris, and hypnoides are found on the mountain
tops. We have not seen S. oppositifolia nearer than
Helvellyn. S. platypetala grows on the heights of Fairfield. Chrysoplenium alternifolium is also found by
some rivulets. Parnassia palustris is very abundant. —
Of Umbelliferæ, Sium angustifolium is common in the
streams, and Myrrhis odorata is by no means rare in
old orchards and elsewhere. — Of Compositæ, Apargia
hispida is common and very handsome. Souchus palustris occurs in some marshy places. Crepis paludosa
is frequent in wet woods. Hieracium alpinum is found
on Langdale Pikes; H. lawsoni, on Kirkstone Pass;
H. inuloides, in mountain rills; H. alpinum is found on
Langdale Pikes; H. murorum and boreale are common;
but we are not able to give a list of all the mountain
species of Hawkweed which may be found in the district; the lower range of fells, near the lake, are not
likely to produce any rare species, but the higher series,
Fairfield, High Street, Hill Bell, &c., would be very likely

to repay a more careful search than has hitherto been made. Serratula tinctoria is plentiful on the shores of the lake. Carduus heterophyllus grows in Troutbeck, Carlina vulgaris on Whitbarrow. Centaurea nigrescens is not unfrequent on dry banks. Bidens cernna is found in Crosthwaite. Eupatorium cannabinum is everywhere common. Graphalium dioicum and sylvaticum are abundant, the former on mountain heaths, the latter in woods. Petastites vulgaris is found in several places. Senecio saracenicus grows near Newby Bridge, and in some old orchards; but it is probably not indigenous. Inula conyza is abundant on the Whitbarrow Fells. — Of Campanulaceæ, C. latifolia is not unfrequent in woody places. Jasione montana everywhere abundant, and the larger form, which has been thought by some to be a distinct species, is often seen in the meadows. Lobelia dortmanna grows in shallow water, in almost every part of the lake. — Of Ericaceæ, Vacinium myrtillus is found in nearly every wood; and V. oxycoccus occurs in a few places. V. vitis-idæa on Langdale Pikes; Pyrola minor in Stockghyll. — Of Jasminaceæ, Ligustrum vulgare grows wild in the mountain woods. Of Gentianaccæ Menyanthes trifoliata is not uncommon in the bogs. Polemonium cæruleum is found in Graythwaite woods. — Of Scrophularianæ, Digitalis purpurea is everywhere most abundant and beautiful, ornamenting every hill and dell with its splendid spikes of purple flowers. Verbena officinalis may be gathered on Whitbarrow. — Of Lamiaceæ, Lycopus europœus is found in a few places, as is also calamintha Clinopodium. Mentha piperita grows on Whitbarrow. M. sativa is

not uncommon throughout the district. Scutellaria
minor occurs in some of the bogs. — Of Boraginaceæ,
Symphytum officinale is not uncommon. — Of Pingui-
culaceæ, Pinguicula vulgaris is very frequent in damp
places. Utricularia vulgaris is also found. Of Pri-
mulaceœ, Primula farinocea may be found in many
moist meadows: it is abundant on Wansfell, and will
be seen when ascending the mountain by Stockghyll.
Lysimachia vulgaris, nummularia and nemorum are
common, the two former by the side of the lake. — Of
Plantaginaceæ, Plantago media is common near Kendal
and on Whitbarrow. Littorella lacustris covers the
margins and bottom of the lake, with a perennial
verdure. — Of Polygonaceæ, Polygonum bistorta is
common and very ornamental in low meadows ; and
Oxyria reniformis is found in Longsleddale. — Of Thy-
melaceæ, Daphne laureola and mezereum have been
found in Rayrigg and Graythwaite woods. — Of Empe-
traceæ, Empetrum nigrum grows on the higher fells. —
Of Amentiferæ, Carpinus betulus is not uncommon, but
probably not indigenous. Salix pentandra occurs in
many places. S. alba, viminalis, caprea and autrita are
common ; but we are not sufficiently acquainted with
this genus to mention all the species found here. — Of
Orchidaceæ, Listera ovata is common, and L. cordata is
found on Helvellyn. Gymnadenia conopsea and Habe-
nara bifolia are very common. Cypripedium calceolus
has been found on Whitbarrow. — Of Amaryllidaceæ
Narcissus pseudo-narcissus is most abundant, and in
early spring makes many a bank and woody glen yellow
with its numerous flowers. — Of Liliaceœ Allium cari-

natum is found in one locality. H. ursinum is very common. H. schœnoprasum may be found on Cartmel Fell. Convallaria majalis grows on some of the islands, but is becoming scarce from too frequent depredations ; in Rauncey woods, about three miles below Newby Bridge, this plant is most abundant and fine, covering some acres of ground ; here also may be found the Fly orchis. C. multiflora abounds in Graythwaite woods, about two miles north of Newby Bridge. — Of Trilliaceœ, Paris quadrifolia is found in many of the shady woods. — Of Alismaceœ, Alisma plantago and ranunculoides are plentiful in the lake. — Of Fluviales, Potamogeton prœlongus is found in many parts of Windermere. P. perfoliatus and heterophyllus are very common. — Of Juncaceœ, Juncus glancus grows on Whitbarrow, and J. triglumis on Fairfield. — Of Cyperaceœ, Eriophorum vaginatum is frequent in mountain bogs. Carex dioica, pulicaris, curta, remota, stricta, prœcox, vesicaria, and ampullacea are common. C. lœvigata and sylvatica are found in some places. — Of Gramina, Avena pubescens, flavescens, are common ; Festuca ovina var, vivipara is found ; Bromus gigantius is very frequent. B. asper on Whitbarrow. Triticum caninum may be seen in many places ; and Melica nutans is found in some moist woods.

Of the Ferns, Ceterach officinarum, occurs on some walls, but is abundant and indigenous on Whitbarrow. Polypodium vulgare, grows very luxuriantly, and in some shaded situations with a south aspect, assumes a form resembling P. canbricum, but does not retain its peculiar character under cultivation ; the variety serra-

tum, also grows in similar situations: it is very handsome. — Polypodium phegopteris is more than usually
common in this district, and may be found in many
woods and often by the road sides. — P. dryopteris is
not quite so frequent, but by no means uncommon in
similar situations; it is very abundant in the woods of
Furness Fells. — Polypodium calcareum is common on
Whitbarrow. — Allosorus crispus is not rare in stone
walls or rocks, and among loose stones, generally
in high situations. — Cystopteris fragilis is very fine in
some situations, but is not abundant here; a form is
found which closely resembles C. regia. — Polystichum
lonchitis has not yet been found nearer than Ullswater.
— P. aculeatum is common by rivulets through mountain woods and coppices, and its varieties lobatum and
lonchitoides. — P. angulare is less common, but may be
found in many warm shady ghylls and groves growing
very luxuriantly. — Lastrea oreopteris is very common.
The different forms of L. dilatata abound; the variety
called by Mr. Newman L. collina, is not rare.—L. spinn-
losa is to be found in many wet woods ; also in some
open bogs, and a few roots of a form of this species closely
resembling, if not identical with L. cristata, have been
found. — L. recurva occurs in a few places. — Athyrium
felix-femina var rhœticum is not uncommon.—Asplenium
viride is found on some of the mountain screes, and is
very abundant on Whitbarrow. A. Trichomanes,
Adiantum-nigrum and ruta-muria are common, and A.
marinum is found on Meathop, near Witherslack.
— Scolopendrium vulgare grows very fine in some
sheltered situations. — Blechnum boreale is common

F

everywhere. — Hymenophyllum Wilsoni is found in
many dark fissures in the rocks in high wooded fells,
generally near a stream. — Osmunda regalis is common
and fine. — Botrychium lunaria is pretty frequent on
high mountain heaths. — Ophioglosum vulgatum is
very scarce. In giving an account of the ferns of
Windermere, the important discovery of Woodsia
Ilvensis in Westmorland, although not in the immediate neighbourhood of Windermere, ought to be mentioned. This rare fern was found by Mr. Huddart, the
nurseryman of Waterloo Gardens immediately opposite
Bowness, who has some roots of it, and of almost all
the British ferns in his possession.

All the British club mosses are found near Windermere Lycopodium clavatum grows on most of the
higher fells. — L. annotinum has been found in Langdale. — L. inundatum is not unfrequent on the margins
of mountain tarns. — L. alpinum grows on many heathy
fell-sides ; L. selago in similar situations ; and L. selagi-
noides is common in rivulets in high situations. —
Isoetes lacustris is abundant in all parts of the lake,
but rather difficult to find, because it is nearly always
in deep water — Equisetum palustre var, polystachyon,
is the only uncommon Horsetail which has hitherto
been found here.

The common Mosses are abundant here, but some
species may be found which are very scarce in Great
Britain, and are only seen in some alpine or sub-alpine
districts. The Muscologist will be delighted with the
general appearance of this tribe of plants, their luxuri-
ance in some situations is truly wonderful. Among

the most rare may be mentioned Zygodon mangestii, in crevices of rocks, without fruit, on Kirkstone. — Gymnostomum rupestre on wet rocks, Helvellyn. — G. Griffithanum on Red Screes, Wrynose and Fairfield. Dyphisicum foliosum on rocks and crevices of rocks, Rydal Park. — Weissia denticulata on rocks, Grasmere Fells. — Grimmia spiralis and torta below Red Screes, Kirkstone, but not in fruit. — Orthotricrum rupincola on walls by Mardale and Haweswater. — O. aristatum on trees in Rydal Park and elsewhere. — Bryum julaceum in mountain rills, fruiting abundantly in Kirkstone Pass and in Wythburn beck. — B. albicans in mountain rills,—B. Ludwigü on wet rocks, Glaramara, not in fruit. — B. zierii in crevices of rocks and on the ground, Red Screes, Rydal Park and elsewhere. — B. Alpinum common, on the mountains, usually barren. — B. uliginosum in a branch of the Wythburn beck, High Raise. — B. accuminatum on the eastern precipices of Fairfield, between the summit and Rydal Head. — B. mnioides on Helvellyn. — Hypnum flagellare in rocky streams, Stockghyll, &c. — H. crista castrensis on banks above Troutbeck Park, by the road over Kirkstone, Dove Craig, Fairfield, Mardale, and Haweswater. Of those mosses which are rare, except in mountainous districts, may be mentioned, as occurring abundantly here, Anictan Qium ciliatum, common on walls and rocks ; Anomodon curtipendulum very common, in some situations bearing fruit abundantly ; Bartramia pomiformis and halleriana are common ; B. arcuata is found at Lowdore ; Hypnum brevirostre is very abundant in woods ; H. undulatum is very fine, and bears fruit in some high woods, generally near waterfalls : Nechera crispa is a great ornament to rather wet rocks ; Polytrichum urnigerum is very common, as are also Trichostomum acciculare, canescens, fasciculare, lanuginosum and poly-phyllum.

A TABLE OF THE HEIGHTS OF MOUNTAINS IN THE COUNTIES
OF CUMBERLAND, WESTMORLAND, AND LANCASHIRE.

No.	Names of Mountains.	Counties.	Height in Feet above the Sea Level.
1	Scawfell Pikes	Cumberland	3166
2	Scawfell ...	,,	3160
3	Helvellyn	,,	3070
4	Skiddaw ...	Westmorland	3022
5	Fairfield	,,	2950
6	Great Gable, Wastdale	Cumberland	2925
7	Bowfell	Westmorland	2914
8	Rydal Head	,,	3910
9	Pillar	Cumberland	2893
10	Blencathra, Saddleback	,,	2787
11	Grassmoor	,,	2756
12	Red Pike, Buttermere	,,	2750
13	High Street, Kentmere	Westmorland	2700
14	Grisedale Pike	Cumberland	2680
15	Coniston Old Man	Lancashire	2576
16	Hill Bell ...	Westmorland	2500
17	Langdale Pikes	,,	2400
18	Carrock Fell, Caldbeck	Cumberland	2110
19	High Pike, Caldbeck ...	,,	2101
20	Causey Pike	,,	2040
21	Black Combe ...	,,	1919
22	Lord's Seat	,,	1728
23	Honister Crag	,,	1700
24	Whinfell Beacon, near Kendal	Westmorland	1500
25	Cat Bell, Newlands	Cumberland	1448
26	Latrigg, Keswick ...	,,	1160

	Height in Feet.
Highest English Mountain, Scawfell Pike, Cumberland	3,166
Highest Welsh Mountain, Snowden, Carnarvonshire	3,571
Highest Irish Mountain, Gurrane Tual, Kerry	3,404
Highest Scotch Mountain, Ben Muedui, Aberdeen	4,418
Highest European Mountain, Mount Blanc	15,718
Highest Mountain in the World, Dhawalagiri, Asia	26,862

PASSES.

		Heights above the Level of the Sea.
Sty Head	Cumberland	... 1250
Buttermere Hawes, Newlands ...	,, ...	1160
Kirkstone	Westmorland	... 1200
Borrowdale Hawes, to Buttermere ...	Cumberland ...	1100
Dunmail Raise...	West. and Cumb.	... 720

F 3

A TABLE OF THE LENGTH, BREADTH, AND DEPTH OF THE LAKES.

No.	Names of Lakes.	Counties.	Length in Miles.	Extreme breadth in Miles.	Extreme depth in Feet.	Height above theSea
1	Windermere	Westmorland	10	1	240	116
2	Haweswater ...	„	3	$\frac{1}{2}$	—	443
3	Grasmere	„	$1\frac{1}{4}$	$\frac{1}{3}$	180	180
4	Brothers Water ...	„	$0\frac{3}{4}$	$\frac{1}{2}$	72	—
5	Rydalwater	„	$0\frac{1}{2}$	$\frac{1}{5}$	54	156
6	Red Tarn, Helvellyn	„	—	—	—	2400
7	Coniston Water ...	Lancashire	6	$\frac{1}{2}$	160	105
8	Esthwaite Water	„	2	$\frac{1}{3}$	80	189
9	Ullswater	Cumberland	9	1	210	380
10	Bassenthwaite Water	„	4	1	68	210
11	Derwentwater... ...	„	3	0	72	228
12	Crummock... ...	„	3	$1\frac{1}{2}$	132	240
13	Buttermere	„	$1\frac{1}{4}$	$\frac{3}{4}$	90	247
14	Loweswater ...	„	1	$\frac{1}{2}$	60	—
15	Ennerdale	„	$2\frac{1}{2}$	$\frac{1}{2}$	80	—
16	Wastwater... ...	„	3	$\frac{1}{2}$	270	160
17	Thirlmere	„	$2\frac{3}{4}$	$\frac{1}{2}$	108	473

WATERFALLS.

No.	Names and Situations of Falls.	Counties.	Feet in the Sea.
1	Colwith Force, five miles from Ambleside	Westmorland	90
2	Dungeon Ghyll Force, Langdale	„	30
3	Stockghyll Force, near Ambleside ...	„	70
4	Rydal Fall, near Ambleside	„	70
5	Scale Force, S. W. Side of Crummock Lake	Cumberland	196
5	Lowdore Cascade, near Keswick... ...	„	150
7	Barrow Cascade, near Keswick	„	122
8	Ara Force, West Side of Ullswater ...	„	80
9	Birker Force, Eskdale...	„	65
10	Stanley Gill, Eskdale	„	62
11	Sour Milk Force, Buttermere	„	60

DIRECTORY.

The address is that required by Postal arrangement; and, Windermere being the head office in the district, should be inserted at the end of each address, to ensure the regular transit of communications from a distance.

WINDERMERE.

Addison, Rev. J. A., St. Mary's Cottage.
Atkinson, James, lodging house, Villa Lodge.
Aufrere, Geo., At. Esq., Burnside.
Ball, James, railway clerk.
Balmer, Grace, laundress, Old Field.
Barrow, R., Elim Grove.
Barrow, R., yeoman, The Grove.
Barrow, John, lodging house, Woodside Cottage.
Beaufoy, Mark, Esq., Bowness Road.
Bell, John, joiner, Elim Grove.
Benson, Mrs., lodging house, Bowness Road.
Benson, W., Esq., Dove's Nest.
Birkett, Mrs., l. house, Elim Grove
Bradford, Earl of, St. Catherine's.
Braithwaite, R., Esq., Elleray.
Brockbank, John, lodging house, Bowness Road.
Brownrigg, John, joiner, Bowness Road.
Bryans, James, Esq., Belfield.
Burnett, Rev Dr., Bowness Road.
Carter, Geo., artist, Elim Grove.

Clowes, Frederic, Esq., surgeon, Holly Hill.
Collinson, Mrs., lodging house, Bowness Road.
Craston, Miles, grocer, Bowness Road.
Crewdson, Geo. B., Esq., Villa Lodge.
Crosthwaite, Samuel, artist, Chapel House, Bowness Road.
Crosthwaite Thomas, yeoman, Birthwaite.
Davies, Mrs., grocer, Church-street.
Dixon, Miss. dressmaker, Bowness Road.
Eastted, William, Esq., Elleray.
Elleray, John, yeoman, Heathwaite.
Fell, Geo., yeoman, Common.
Field, John, Esq., Cross-street.
Fleming, John, farmer, Ecclerigg.
Fletcher, John, Esq., Craig Foot.
Gandy, John, Esq., Ellergrange.
Garnett, John, railway superintendant, — Printer, bookseller, &c., Post Office.

Garnett, Miss, milliner, High-street.

Gardner, Geo. H., Esq., solicitor, Ellerthwaite.

Greaves, Mrs., Ferney Green.

Greaves, Rev., Robert P., Dove Nest.

Greg, Wm. R., Esq., The Craig.

Gregg, B., cordwainer, Elim Grove.

Harrison, Wm., joiner, High-st.

Harrison, Mrs., Fancy Repository, High-street.

Hayton, John, joiner and grocer, Bowness Road.

Hayton, Richard, lodging house keeper & joiner, Bowness Road.

Herd, Thomas, grocer, Bowness Road.

Holmes, John, grocer, High-st.

Hornby, Rev., Jas. J., Wansfell.

Holmes, Wm., surgeon, Cleator Lodge.

Hutchinson, Isaac, farmer, Common.

Jones, Robert, Esq., Elim Grove.

Kennedy, Peter, Esq., Fair View.

Logan, Robert, Low Wood Hotel.

Longmire, J., farmer, Banrigg.

Longmire, R., butcher, Lickbarrow.

Lowe, Myles, grocer, Old-road.

Macdougall, Mrs., North View.

Marriott, Miss, St. Mary's Abbey.

Martin, Nicholas, railway porter.

Medcalf, Richard, waller.

Melville, Thomas, agent, Storrs.

Meyer, Miss, Holbeck Cottage.

Mitchell, Robert, blacksmith, Cross-street.

Mounsey, George, slater, Elim Grove.

Mounsey, W., joiner, Cross-street.

Newby, James, gardener, Elleray.

Parrington, J., farmer, Dromer.

Pattinson, Miss Betty, Woodland Grove.

Pattinson, Abraham, builder, Elim Grove.

Pattinson, John, lodging house, Elim Grove.

Pearson, Mrs., Briery Close.

Postlethwaite, Robert, joiner, Bowness Road.

Richardson, Stephen, Village Inn.

Rigg, Richard, Windermere Hotel.

Salkeld, James, cordwainer, High-street.

Scholes, Mrs. Annesdale.

Sheldon, Wm., coach proprietor, Highfield.

Sockett, T., grocer, Elim Grove.

Somervell, Robert M., Esq.

Staniforth, Rev. Thomas, Storrs Hall.

Sternberg, Baroness de, Belsfield.

Swinburne, Edward, Esq., Calgarth Park.

Tallon, Miss, confectioner, Bowness Road.

Taylor, John H., Esq., solicitor.

Taylor, Samuel, Esq., (J.P.) Ibbotsholme.

Taylor, John, corn merchant.

Thompson, J., joiner, Cross-st.

Ullock, Thomas, Esq., Quarry How.

Warwick, Thomas, blacksmith, Bowness Road.

Watson, Miss, Mylnbeck.

Watson, R. Luther, Esq., Ecclerigg.

Wilson, J., farmer, Cooks House.

Wilson, Capt., R.N., (J.P.) The Howe.

Wilkinson, Rev., J. H., Rectory.

Wright, Henry, lodging house, Bowness Road.

Yates, Miss Jane, The Wood.

BOWNESS.

Airey, John, farmer, Cleabarrow.
Allen, Oswald, grocer and draper.
Armstrong, David, museum.
Atkinson, John, grocer & draper.
Atkinson, James, saddler.
Atkinson, J., waller, Millbeck Stock.
Backhouse, J., beerhouse keeper.
Balmer, Michael, lodging house.
Barker, H., tailor and draper.
Barrow, James, joiner.
Barrow, Roger, grocer, Langdale View.
Barrow, R. yeoman.
Battersby, Thomas, gardener.
Battersby, Thomas. joiner.
Beetham, Ann, dressmaker.
Belcher, Lucy, bazaar.
Benson, Robert
Birkett, J., Esq., Birkett Houses.
Birkett, W., gardener.
Blaylock, William, grocer
Bownass, William, Royal Hotel.
Brockbank, William, carter.
Burton, Thomas, tailor.
Butcher, Mrs.
Cloudsdale, Thos., Crown Hotel.
Collinson, John, Esq., Brantfell.
Crosthwaite, Joseph, joiner.
Crosthwaite, John, grocer.
Curwen, Henry, Esq., Belle Isle.
Dickinson, R., farmer, Winster.
Dickinson, R., Belfield Farm.
Dickinson, J., lodging house.
Dixon, Thomas, yeoman, Belmanground.
Dobson, William, blacksmith, lodginghouse keeper.
Dobson, J., blacksmith.
Eccles, Thomas, post-messenger.
Eccles, R., joiner.
Eglin, George T., Winster.
Elleray, Stephen, Winster.

Elleray, T., Winster.
Fisher, James, lodging house.
Fletcher, Joseph, cabinetmaker.
Garnett, Edward, land agent.
Garnett, T., Esq., High Mill.
Gawith, John, carrier.
Gibson, G. Henry, Esq.
Gill, Dawson, ostler.
Gregg, George, carrier.
Gregg, Reginald, grocer.
Hadwin, J., cordwainer.
Harrison, J., beerhouse keeper.
Harrison, W., Brantfell.
Hartley, Thomas.
Heaps, Thomas, lodging house.
Herdson, J., High House.
Hiley, M., musician.
Hoggarth, Mary.
Holmes, Miss, milliner.
Howlett, Rev., Fred., Winster.
Huddleston, J., tailor & draper.
Jacob, Lieut. Colonel, Rayrigg.
Kendall, George, painter.
Kirkbride, Charles.
Ladyman, Geo., schoolmaster.
Livesey, Joseph, Esq., Green Bank.
Longmire, Thomas, beerhouse.
Long, Miss, milliner.
Martin, John, beerhouse keeper.
Martin, Wilson, painter, &c.
Martin, Mrs., innkeeper.
Martindale, W., farmer, Barker Knot.
Mattix, Mrs. Berlin Wool Repository.
Millray, M. H., gardener, Belsfield.
Molesworth, Lieutenant, R.N., Waterside Cottage.
Moon, James, yeoman.
Moon, Tobias, basket maker, Belman Houses.

Parker, Miss, milliner.
Postlethwaite, Woodburn, Esq., solicitor, Matson House.
Redman, John, lodging house.
Reed, Christopher, carrier.
Reid, Robert, sadler.
Richardson, T., farmer, Helm.
Richmond, John T., painter.
Rigg, Ellen.
Robinson, Agnes.
Robinson, Agnes, Fell Side.
Robinson, Ann, glass dealer.
Robinson, Robert, cordwainer.
Robinson, R.James, lodg. house.
Robinson, Miss, lodging house, Howe Villa.
Robinson, Thomas, tailor.
Robinson, Wlliam, waller.
Robinson, G., lodging house.
Robinson, John, Lindeth.
Robinson, W., Lindeth.
Rubottom, Margaret, grocer.
Sabin, George, lodging house.
Sandham, John, beerhouse keeper
Scott, James, Victoria Hotel.
Searle, H., lodging house.
Sewell, Mrs., Fallbarrow.
Shaw, T., gardener.
Shrigly, Miss, Langdale View.
Sill, John, flour & butter dealer.
Sowerby, Luke, basket maker.

Stables, W., farmer.
Stewardson, R., beerhouse keeper
Stewardson, John, gardener.
Stockdale, E., lodging house.
Stringer, John, lodging house.
Stringer, Henry, druggist.
Suart, Thomas, b. h., Brow Top.
Suart, William, junr., auctioneer.
Swainson, William, schoolmaster, Winster.
Taylor, B., shoemaker, Winster.
Taylor, J., farmer, Low House.
Taylor, T., boat builder, Low House.
Turner, R., basket maker, Mill-beck Stock.
Walker, A., beerhouse keeper.
Walker, Thomas, lodging house.
Ward, Fredrick, Esq., Gill Head.
Waters, George, ironmonger.
Webber, Lieut., R.N., Old England.
Wharton, J., hair-dresser.
Wildman and Holmes, joiners and builders.
Wilkinson, William, blacksmith.
Wilson, Robert, farmer, Miller-ground.
Wright, W. James, Windy Hall.
Wood, Jos., Temperance Hotel.
Wood, Robert, beerhouse keeper.

NEWBY BRIDGE.

Ainsworth, T., Esq., cotton manufacturer, Backbarrow.
Astley, F. D. P., Esq., Fell Foot.
Backhouse, Simpson, farmer, Finsthwaite.
Bateman, Thomas, Beck Hire, beerhouse keeper and farmer.
Bigland, Rev., John, Esq., Finsthwaite.
Braithwaite, Thomas beerhouse keeper, Finsthwaite.

Burns, James, farmer, Back-barrow.
Carter, John, grocer, Staveley,
Carter, William, hoop maker and farmer, Finsthwaite.
Crow, Mark, farmer, Graith-waite.
Cormic, William, Esq,, Cunsey.
Dixon, W., farmer, Cunsey,
Fell, John, Esq., Stott Park.
Fell, John, farmer, Finsthwaite,

Fleming, Daniel, Newby Bridge Mill.
Fell, John, blacksmith.
Fell, Christopher, bobbin manufacturer, Cunsey.
Harrison, John, farmer and basket maker.
Ainslie Harrison and Co., Iron Works, Backbarrow.
Harrison, Mrs., Landing.
Kellett, Wm., carter, Landing.
Kirkby, James, grocer & butcher, Backbarrow.
Kirkbride, Robert, farmer, Finsthwaite.
Lewthwaite, G., Esq., Stott Park.
Martin, Joseph, farmer and land agent, Blakeholmes.
Pedder, John, Esq., Finsthwaite House.
Preston, William, farmer, Town End.

Revley, M., farmer, Graithwaite.
Rowlandson, Joshua, quarryman, Town Ward.
Rowlandson, James, yeoman, Backbarrow.
Sandys, J. D., Esq., Graithwaite.
Steele, Christopher, shoemaker, Backbarrow.
Swainson, John, yeoman, Helm Well, Cunsey.
Swainson, Jos., farmer and hoop maker, Cunsey.
Turner, J., farmer, Finsthwaite.
Townley, W., Esq., Town Head.
Robinson, William, farmer, Stott Park.
Welsh, Richard, coal dealer, Backbarrow.
Wharton, W. bobbin manufacturer, Stott Park.
White Thomas, Swan Hotel.
Wren, John, joiner and builder.

SAWREY.

Arnold, James, Ferry Hotel.
Aspland, T. Lindsey, Esq., artist, Sawrey Cottage.
Atkinson, E., hoop maker, Satter How.
Atkinson, John, Spout House.
Brooks, J. N., schoolmaster.
Carradus, Barrow, farmer, Spout Mire.
Carradus, M., farmer, Harrow Slack.
Clark, Thomas, farmer, Satter How.
Cowburn, Mrs., Chapel Cottage.
Dixon, J., grocer, Post Office.
Forrest, George, farmer, Briers.
Forrest, John, yeoman, Low House.
Forrest, Mrs. Henry, widow.

Garnett, Joseph, Esq., Howend Cottage.
Halstead, W., Esq., Mount Cottage.
Hartley, Richard, New Inn.
Hawkrigg, T., blacksmith.
Hawkrigg, Braithwaite, yeoman.
Hawkrigg, Hugh, yeoman, Castle.
Herdson, William, butcher.
Huddart, J., seedsman, Waterloo Gardens.
Jackson, G., farmer, Eelhouse.
Ogden, Jonathan, R. Esq., (J.P.) Lake Field.
Preston, William, farmer, Hill Top.
Smith, William, hoop maker.
Smith, Elizabeth, grocer.
Stalker, John, grocer.

Stalker, Jonathan, beerhouse keeper.
Stalker, Jonathan, basket maker.
Stalker, W., boatman.
Taylor, Joseph, yeoman, Buckle Yeat.

Taylor, Thomas, shoemaker.
Taylor, J. joiner.
Towers, W., yeoman, Towerbank.
Towers, Mrs., Sawrey House.
Willan, Thos., spirit merchant.
Willison, Ann, schoolmistress.

TROUTBECK.

Beaumont, Thos., farmer, Crag.
Benson, Anthony, yeoman, Coat Syke.
Benson, William, farmer, Low Longmire.
Benson, Thomas, yeoman, High Green.
Benson, John, yeoman, Crosses.
Bigland, John, farmer, Near Borrans.
Birkett, William, yeoman, Town Head.
Birkett, George, Brow Head.
Birkett, Thomas, yeoman, Great House.
Birkett, Robert, yeoman, Middleriggs.
Braithwaite, James, yeoman, Town Foot.
Braithwaite, Elizabeth, schoolmistress, Mathew How.
Braithwaite, John, mechanic, Troutbeck Bridge.
Brownrigg, George, joiner, Beckside Cottage.
Browne, Harrison, yeoman, Drummermer Head.
Browne, Mrs. Lucy, Town End.
Browne, Richard, farmer, Low Wood.
Browne, Ben., yeoman, Boot.
Coffee, Jeremiah, tailor, Crag.
Dawson, Mrs., Crag House.
Fell, Robert H., bobbin maker, Troutbeck Bridge.

Forrest, Birkett, yeoman, Low Fold.
Forrest, Matthew, farmer, Low Skelgill.
Gandy, Henry, Esq., Troutbeck Park.
Green, Elizabeth, innkeeper, Mortal Man.
Harrison, Thomas, schoolmaster, Crag.
Hayton, George, joiner, Town Head.
Holme, Edward, blacksmith, Troutbeck Bridge.
Hunter, Thomas, farmer, Town Head.
Hutchinson, John, Esq., Broad Oaks.
Jenkinson, Thomas, yeoman, Near Orrest.
Kennedy, Simon, letter carrier.
Lancaster, J., innkeeper, Kirkstone Top.
Lancaster, Henry, bootmaker, Longmire Gate.
Lancaster, Thomas, bootmaker, Lane.
Leather, Thomas, tailor & draper, Mathew How.
Longmire, Jas., farmer, Orrest.
Longmire, W., churchwarden, Crosses.
Longmire, John, yeoman, Longmire.
Longmire, J., farmer, Longmire.

Mackereth, Benson, innkeeper, Queen's Head.
Mackereth, W., yeoman, High Fold.
Mounsey, William, relieving-officer, and registrar of births and deaths, Highfold.
Pool, Jos., yeoman, Slack Foot.
Pool, Abram, yeoman, Beckside.
Rigg, George, blacksmith, Longmire Gate.
Sewell, Rev., William, Low Fold.
Stainton, Thomas, farmer, Town Head.
Storey, Thomas, yeoman, High Green.
Storey, Alison, farmer, Lane Foot.

Storey, Geo., waller, Lane Foot.
Storey, Christopher, farmer, High Fold.
Storey, John, farmer, Limefit.
Todd, George, farmer, Longgreen Head.
Todd, James, farmer, Crag.
Townson, Richard, farmer, Midtown.
Tyson, Henry, innkeeper, Troutbeck Bridge. — Post Office.
Tyson, Thomas, farmer, High Skelgill.
Tyson, Isaac, farmer, Town Head.
Wilson, Nicholas, yeoman, Town End.
Wilson, Nicholas, junr., farmer, Town End.

AMBLESIDE.

Abbot, John, coach office and lodging house, Fairfield,
Arnold, Mrs., widow of the late Dr. Arnold, Fox How.
Atkinson, James, joiner, Fisher Beck.
Atkinson, J., saddler, market-place.
Backhouse, M., schoolmistress, New Road.
Backhouse, James, farmer and lodging house keeper, Rydal.
Ball, William, Esq., Glen Rothay.
Barrow, John, farmer, Hawkshead Hill.
Barwick, John, surgeon.
Barwick, Thomas, carpenter.
Barrow, John, joiner.
Barton, Mrs., milliner.
Barton, William, schoolmaster.
Barkworth, Alfred, Esq., Tranby Lodge,
Beck, James, farmer, Mire Side, Skelwith.

Bell, Catherine, stay maker.
Bell, R. F., ironmonger.
Bell, Thomas, chemist and druggist.
Benson, Henry, blacksmith, Blue Hill.
Black, Anne, Golden Rule Inn.
Bonney, Richard, plumber.
Brenchley, Alexander C., Esq., Wanlas How.
Brown, John, Commercial Hotel, Excise Office.
Brocklebank, Benjamin, farmer, Stang End.
Carr, Thomas, Esq., Hill Top.
Carter, John, Esq., Rydal Mount.
Clark, Miles, grocer.
Claude, Mrs. L., Broadlands.
Claude, Mrs. A., Rose Cottage.
Clay, Rev. J., Miller Bridge.
Cleminson, James, solicitor.
Clough, Mrs., Ladies' Seminary, Eller How.
Conway and Henshall, milliners.

Cookson, Miss, Clappersgate.
Cookson, Isaac, boot and shoe maker.
Cousins, Henry, joiner.
Coward, John, joiner and lodging house keeper, Beech Cottage.
Coward, William, tailor & draper.
Coward, Jeremiah, painter.
Coward, Jeremiah, innkeeper, miller, & grocer, Skelwith Bridge.
Coward, John, bobbin manufacturer, Skelwith Bridge.
Cowperthwaite, George, farmer, Clappersgate.
Coward, Mrs., lodging house.
Creighton, John, yeoman, Low Park.
Creighton, Joseph, blacksmith.
Crewdson, Wm. Dil., Esq., Field Foot.
Crosley, John, farmer, Hawkshead Hill.
Crosfield, John, Esq., Rothay Bank.
Davy, John, Esq., M.D., Lesketh How.
Dawson, Thomas, waller.
Dawson, James, Esq., (J.P.) Wray Castle.
Dawson, Miss, Randy Pike.
Dawson, Daniel, farmer, High Park.
Dickinson, Miss, Nook End.
Dobson, Mrs., lodging house, Prospect Cottage.
Donaldson, Peter, Salutation Hotel.
Dove, Charles, farmer, Low Fold.
Dowling, Miss, Hill Top.
Fell, Rev. S. I., Sweeden How.
Fell, William, Esq., surgeon.
Fisher, Robert, lodging house, Stock Cottage.
Fleming, Mark, boot and shoe maker.

Fleming, Rev. Fletcher, incumbent, Rydal Lodge.
Fleming, Lady le, Rydal Hall.
Fleming, Mrs., draper & milliner.
Fleming, Roger, joiner.
Forrest, Mrs., lodging house, Windermere Lodge.
Foster, Miss, Wray Cottage.
Frearson, Rev. S., baptist minister, Hawkshead Hill.
Gibson, Mrs., grocer.
Gibson, William, tallow chandler.
Gill, Miss, Oak Bank.
Grave, Mrs., Oxenfell.
Green, Mrs., Gale cottage.
Green, James, butcher and lodging house keeper, Fisher Beck.
Grier, John, florist and seedsman.
Hodgson, John, farmer, Hawkshead Hill.
Harrison, Matthew B., Esq., (J.P.) Belle View.
Harrison, John, Esq., The Green.
Harrison, Mrs., lodging house, Chapel Cottage.
Harrison, Benson, Esq., (J.P.) Scale How.
Hawley, Cpt. R., Rock Cottage.
Hawkrigg, Michael, mason.
Hawkrigg, James, yeoman, Skelwith.
Hawkrigg, Joseph, farmer, Park House, Skelwith.
Hayse, Robert, gardener and seedsman.
Head, Miss, Compston Lodge.
Herd, Edward, watch maker.
Higgins, Miss, Fancy Repository.
Hodgson, Rev., William, Old Brathay.
Holme, John, tailor.
Holme, William, bread baker.
Holme, Thomas, blacksmith.
Holme, James, Esq., Croft Lodge, Clappersgate.

Hopkinson, Benjamin, Esq., The Oaks.

Horrax, Charles, bobbin manufacturer.

Irving, Mrs., lodging house keeper Rydal.

Irving, William, cooper, Hawkshead Hill.

Jackson, Mrs., Waterhead House.

Jackson, Henry, Royal Oak Inn.

Jackson, Mrs., Newfield Cottage.

Jackson, Thomas, carter and coal agent.

Jackson, Arthur, mason, Rose Cottage.

Jenkinson, W., bread baker.

Jameson, Miss, Smithy Brow.

Johnson, Mrs. E., lodging house, Chapel Hill.

Lancaster, Mary, butcher.

Leighton, George, plumber, &c.

Lutwidge, Capt. H., R.N., The Cottage.

Mackereth, Thomas, farmer.

Martin, Richard, lodging house keeper, Chapel Hill.

Martineau, Miss, H., The Knoll.

Matty, Robert, tailor & draper.

Mayson, Bryan, plasterer and lodging house.

Morse, Miss, Gale Lodge.

Mundull, Thomas, tax collector, Loughrigg.

Nelson, Christopher, draper.

Newby, James, draper, Bank.

Newton, George Law, wine and spirit merchant, Waterhead.

Newton, Mrs. Mary, Waterhead.

Newton, Mary, draper and milliner.

Nicholson, John, Esq., solicitor.

Nicholson, Mrs., Agnes, stationer, Post Office.

Noble, James, painter.

Okell, Miss, Sweeden Bank.

Parker, John, slate merchant, Hodge Close.

Partridge, George, Esq., Covey Cottage.

Pedder, Mrs., Gale House.

Piell, William, hooper, cooper, and grocer.

Pritchard, Mrs., bread baker.

Preston, Thomas, farmer, Mill Brow, Skelwith Bridge.

Proctor, John, lodging house, Hill Side Cottage.

Quillinan, Misses, Loughrigg Holme.

Redmayne, Giles, Esq., Brathay Hall.

Reynolds, M., Esq., Clappersgate.

Richards, John, boot and shoe maker.

Ridgway, Mrs., Low Field.

Richardson, William, carrier and farmer, Rydal.

Riddle, Mrs., lodging house, Five-ways House.

Robinson, William, flag merchant, Blue Hill.

Robinson, Messrs., M. & J. C., carriers.

Robinson, Brian, farmer, Rock Cottage.

Roberts, Christopher, farmer, Ellers Brow, Skelwith.

Robinson, John, Esq., Gunpowder Works, Elterwater.

Robinson, Mason, clerk, Gunpowder Works, Elterwater.

Rogers, Major, Pull Cottage.

Rollinshaw, Anthony, boot and shoe maker & l. house keeper.

Roughsedge, Hornby, Esq., (J.P.) Fox Ghyll.

Salkeld, William, farmer, Skelwith Fold.

Sarginson, James, farmer, Skelwith.

Sarginson, Mr., lodging house, Skelwith Bridge.

Shepherd, James, Esq., surgeon.

Slee, Lancelot, farmer, Arnside.

Slater, Mrs., confectioner and lodging house.

Sproat, John, accountant and lodging house, Fairfield.

Sproat, William, boot and shoe maker.

Squires, Mrs., glass dealer and hair dresser.

Stables, Edward, saddler.

Stalker, Betsy, grocer.

Stalker, Mrs., A., Springfield.

Stansfield, Mrs., Waterhead.

Suart, James, Esq., Low Fold.

Tatham, Rev. J., curate, Rydal.

Thompson, Jackson, joiner and lodging house, Waterhead.

Thompson, Joseph, boat builder.

Thompson, John, painter.

Thompson, Jonathan, grocer.

Thompson, Miss, lodging house, Walton Cottage.

Thwaite, Joseph, bread baker.

Townson, William, White Lion Hotel.

Townson, Thomas, miller.

Townson, Benjamin, tax collector, Woodbine Cottage.

Townley, Robert, Unicorn Inn.

Troughton, Thomas, bookseller, &c., Stamp Office.

Troughton, Miss D., lodging house.

Tyson, Thomas, farmer, Waterhead.

Tyson, Joseph, carpenter.

Tyson, Joseph, confectioner.

Walton, Edward, shoemaker.

Walker, John, grocer and confectioner.

Wilson, John, Esq., solicitor, Cross Brow.

Wilson, Thomas, Esq., Clappersgate.

Woodburn, John, grocer and game dealer.

Woodburn, Mrs., lodging house.

Woodhouse, Richard, gardener, Haven Cottage.

Woof, Mrs., farmer, Low Fold.

Woodend, John, farmer, Nook End.

Wordsworth, Mrs., widow of the late Wm. Wordsworth, Rydal Mount.

CONISTON.

Atkinson, Thomas, Waterhead Hotel.

Barnett, George, innkeeper.

Barratt, William, Hollyhow Cottage.

Barratt, John, Esq., Holyworth House.

Barrow, Edward, Black Bull Inn.

Barrow, Joseph, yeoman, Little Arrow.

Barrow, William, yeoman, Outrake.

Barrow, Henry, yeoman, Heathwaite.

Barrow, Adam, farmer, Cat Bank.

Barrow, William, farmer, Heathwaite.

Burrow, George, farmer and wool stapler, Hallgarth.

Beever, the Misses, Thwaite.

Bell, William, joiner, Hawsbank.

Benson, John, farmer, Yew Tree.

Boileau, Simon John, Esq., Parsonage.

Bowdin, Daniel, accountant.

Bownass, Wm., yeoman, Brow.

Bownass, Roger, yeoman, Dixon Ground.

Bownass, George, junr.,

Bownass, Roger, grocer and draper, Post Office.

Briggs, John, carrier.

Briggs, John, junr., carrier.

Bywater, R. T., Esq., surgeon.

Chambre, Miss, Bank Ground.

Collinson, William, farmer, Low Yewdale.

Coward, Edward, farmer, Farend.

Coward, Henry, grocer & carrier, Bridge End.

Coward, Edward, joiner, Saw Mills.

Diddams, John, school master.

Dixon, Benjamin, yeoman, Spoon Hall.

Dixon, William, yeoman, Dixon Ground.

Dodgson, George, grocer &c., Bridge End.

Dixon, Joseph, grocer.

Dixon, John, tailor.

Fleming, George, butcher, Yewdale Bridge.

Fleming, John, shoemaker.

Fleming, Robert, blacksmith.

Gaskgarth, Anthony, lodg. house.

Grave, William, Railway Tavern.

Hall, Joseph, grocer.

Harker, James, Rising Sun, beerhouse.

Irving, Isaac, farmer, Coniston Hall.

Jackson, John, farmer, High Yewdale.

Jackson, Edward, farmer and slate merchant, Tilberthwaite.

Knight, John, farmer and assessment overseer.

Knipe, Thomas & James, tailors.

Linton, William J., artist, Brantwood.

Marshall, J. G., Esq., M.P., Waterhead House.

Massicks, Isaac, Crown Hotel.

Massicks, Isaac, blacksmith.

Mason, Miles, yeoman & waller, Low Houses.

Mossop, Clement, tailor.

Milligan, George, farmer, Tarn Haws.

Nicholson, Elleanor, grocer.

Parker, John, farmer and slate merchant, Holme Ground.

Pickles, Richard, farmer, Dixon Ground.

Poole, John, butcher.

Prickett, Richard, farmer, Dixon Ground.

Redhead, Edward, painter and glazier.

Romney, William, agent to J. G. Marshall, Esq.

Shuttleworth, Joseph, farmer, Tent Lodge.

Shuttleworth, Wilson, butcher, Waterhead.

Smith, James Andrew, Esq., Admiralty Office, Bank Ground.

Smith, Wordsworth, Esq., Coniston Bank.

Smith, Mrs., Coniston Bank.

Spedding, John, yeoman, Bowmanstead,

Stolzman, Lieut. Col., Polish Exile.

Thwaites, William, shoemaker.

Tolming, Rev. Thomas, incumbent of Coniston.

Towers, Matthew, yeoman, Little Arrow.

Townson, William, yeoman Gill.

Tyson, George, tailor and draper.

Tyson, Joseph, yeoman, High Ground.

G

Walker, Henry, farmer, Bank Ground.

Wilson, Wm., yeoman, Beckses.

Wilson, Matthew, yeoman, Hollins Bank.

Wilson, John, carrier.

Wilson, Thomas, farmer, Coniston Bank.

Wilson, John, farmer, Rowlandson Ground.

Wilson, Wm., beerhouse keeper, Miners Arms.

GRASMERE.

Airey, James, post master, Under How.

Agar, Miss, Orrell's Cottage.

Atkinson, Thomas, shoemaker.

Brown, Edward, auctioneer and appraiser, Hollins Hotel.

Brocklebank, Edward, farmer, Underhelm.

Collis, A. P., artist, Belle Vue.

Cookson, Thomas, farmer and lodging house keeper, Dale End

Cookson, Mrs., How Foot.

Cowperthwaite, William, lodging house keeper, Church Stile.

Dixon, James, farmer & builder, Bove Beck.

Fleming, Rev. Sir Richard, rector, Rectory.

Fleming, James, yeoman, Knott's Houses.

Fleming, John, provision dealer, Knott's Houses.

Farquhar, Lady, Dale Cottage.

Fletcher, Mrs., Lankrigg.

Fleming, John yeoman, Under How.

George, W. P., artist, Rose Cottage.

Gibson, Mrs., Kelbarrow.

Gibson, Miss. St. Oswalds.

Green, John, Esq., Pavement End.

Green, John, Esq., land agent, Rylands.

Green, William, yeoman, Beck Allans.

Greenwood, J. Y., Esq., Wyke.

Green, Daniel, provision dealer, Pavement End.

Harrison, Thomas, farmer and carrier, Gill Foot.

Hayton, Robert, farmer, Score Cragg.

Heelis, Stephen, Esq., solicitor, Forrest Side.

Hodgson, Levi, waller & builder, Town End.

Hodgson, Peter, boot and shoe maker, Town End.

Jefferies, Rev. Edward, curate, Allan Bank.

Jenkinson, Daniel, farmer, Goody Bridge.

Johnson, Rev. William, Silver How.

Luff, Mrs., Dale Cottage.

Mackereth, David, parish clerk, Wyke.

Mackereth, Gawin, boatman and guide, Town End.

Phillips, Captain, The Wray.

Postlethwaite, Jos., blacksmith, White Bridge.

Rothery, Mary, farmer, Goody Bridge.

Sandford, Thomas, Esq., Ben Place.

Scott, William, general trader, Swan Inn.

Usher, Isaac, Red Lion Hotel.

Walker, Isaac, farmer, Broad Rain.

Walker, Ed., grocer, Moss Side.
Walker, Edward, blacksmith, Town End.
Wilson, J., yeoman, Goody Bridge.

Wilson, Edward & Sons, builders, Stubdale Cottage.
Wilson, John, builder, &c., Butterlep How.

HAWKSHEAD.

Atkinson, Robert, police officer.
Atkinson, John, grocer.
Atkinson, John, hoop manufacturer, Outgate.
Atkinson, Richard B., beerhouse keeper, Outgate.
Backhouse, Richard, farmer, High Wray.
Bainbridge, Mrs., Sarah.
Baisbrown, John, gardener and seedsman.
Baisbrown, Richard, earthenware dealer.
Bardsley, Thomas, schoolmaster.
Barker, John, painter & glazier.
Beck, Mrs., Esthwaite Lodge.
Bell, Anthony, yeoman, Birkrey.
Bell, Dorothy, tea dealer, Green End.
Benson, Thomas, farmer, Field Head.
Black, George, farmer, Atwood.
Bowman, Thomas, Esq., (J.P.) Rogerground.
Bownass, George, waller, Waterside.
Bownass, William, calf dealer, Thompson Ground.
Braithwaite, George, boot and shoe maker.
Braithwaite, William, plasterer.
Brockbank, Robert & Matthew, joiners, Hannakin.
Burton, John, tailor and draper.
Chapman, Ann, Hill Top.
Coward, James, sadler.
Coward, Rev. William, schoolmaster.

Coward, Edward, farmer, Keen Ground.
Coward, William, miller, Hawkshead Mill.
Coward, William, flag merchant, Outgate.
Crawford, Rev. Samuel, Borwick Lodge.
Croasdale, John, farmer, Skinner How.
Croasdale, Isabella, farmer, Sawrey Ground.
Dixon, James, waller, Croft Head.
Dowbiggin, James, auctioneer.
Dowbiggin, John, joiner.
Dugdale, Richard, farmer, Cragg
Dugdale, John, farmer, Tock How.
Forrest, William, farmer, Beyont Field.
Forsyth, John, wood monger, Field Head.
Fothergill, John, farmer, Esthwaite Hall.
Garnett, Mary, Borwick Ground.
Garnett, George, farmer, Sunny Brow.
Gibson, Alexander Craig, surgeon.
Gill, Sarah, King's Arms Inn.
Green, Samuel, clerk and sexton.
Hale, Miss Elizabeth, dressmaker
Hartley, William, bacon dealer and farmer, Tock How.
Hawkrigg, John, yeoman, Town End.
Hetherington, Sarah, oat bread baker.

G 2

Hewitson, Miles, boot and shoe maker.

Hickie, Daniel Banfield, L.L.D., master of grammar school.

Hodgson, Braithwaite, Esq., Green End.

Hodgson, William, blacksmith, Gallowbarrow.

Hopkins, Joseph, Esq., Belle Grange.

Hudson, Rich., farmer, Birkrey.

Huish, Calverley, Esq.

Hutchinson, John, boot and shoe maker.

Hutchinson, Margaret, confectioner.

Jackson, Richard, Sun Inn.

Jefferson, William, farmer, Borwick Lodge.

Keen, Jacob, farmer, Howe.

Kendall, Wm., yeoman Hawkshead Field.

Kendall, James, yeoman, Hawkshead Field.

Kilner, Mrs., Richmond Villa.

Kirkby, Ruth, farmer, Waterson Ground.

Kirkby, Robert, auctioneer, Colthouse.

Ladyman, George, Queen's Head Inn.

Leviston, George S., yeoman, Greystone Cottage.

Lodge, Edmund, Esq., Keen Ground.

Martin, John, hoop manufacturer

Martin, George, waller.

Medcalf, William, Esq., Mill Hill Cottage.

Milligan, Joseph, farmer, Castle.

Milligan, Michael, farmer, Knipe Fold.

Newby, John, farmer, Foldyeat

Nicholson, George, tailor and draper,

Noble, Robert, boot and shoe maker.

Noble, the Misses, drapers.

Noble, Mary, confectioner.

Noble, John, ironmonger and grocer.

Park, Rev. George, Parsonage, Walker Ground.

Park, William, joiner.

Park, James, swiller, Gallowbarrow.

Park, John, farmer, Dodgsonground.

Parker, Anthony, farmer, Hawkshead Hall.

Poole, John, butcher, Rogerground.

Poole, John, Esq., solicitor, Field Head House.

Postlethwaite, Isaac, tailor.

Proctor, John, grocer.

Purdie, James, tin plate worker.

Raven, Mrs., Walker Ground.

Raven, Robert, sadler.

Rigg, John, clogger, Outgate.

Robinson, Thomas, vet. surgeon.

Rowlandson, Margaret, spinster.

Rowlandson, John, gentleman.

Satterthwaite, Thomas, cooper, Outgate.

Satterthwaite, Thomas, farmer, Loanthwaite.

Satterthwaite, Jonathan, bacon curer, Colthouse.

Satterthwaite, Wm., blacksmith.

Satterthwaite, Jane, spinster.

Scales, Rowland, yeoman, Outgate.

Scott, John, Carrier.

Scott, Miss Deborah, dressmaker.

Slater and Heelis, solicitors.

Steele, Jonathan, yeoman.

Studdart, Robert, boot and shoe maker.

Swainson, G,, farmer, Sike Side.

Taylor, John, relieving officer.
Taylor, Ann, grocer.
Taylor, George, plasterer.
Taylor, Ferdinando, Red Lion Inn.
Taylor, the Misses, milliners and dressmakers.
Taylor, Rev. Robert, schoolmaster Hannakin.
Taylor, Isaac, blacksmith, Hannakin.
Taylor, Joseph, beerhouse keeper, Waterbarnets.
Usher, John, Brown Cow Inn.
Usher, Benjamin, waller, Hannakin.
Usher, John, waller, Sand Ground.
Walker, Thomas, carpenter, Gallowbarrow.
Walker, Mary, grocer, Gallowbarrow.

Walker, William, bobbin manufacturer, Bobbin Mill Cottage.
Walker, John Thomas, bobbin turner, Summer Hill.
Wardley, Joshua, farmer, High House.
Wardley, Thomas, farmer, High Barn.
Warriner, T., yeoman, Outgate.
Watson, Charles, postmaster.
Watson, Gawn, tallow chandler.
Watson, Anne, draper.
Whittaker, Rev. Doctor, Belmount.
Wilkinson, William, excise officer.
Wilson, Mary, national school mistress.
Wilson, John, carrier.
Wilcock, Thomas, Esq., Lake Bank.
Wilson, William, Esq., land agent, High Wray.

BOWNESS, LAKE WINDERMERE.

ULLOCK'S ROYAL HOTEL,

(Late White Lion.)

THE OLDEST ESTABLISHED HOTEL IN THE DISTRICT.

W. BOWNASS,

PROPRIETOR OF THE ABOVE HOTEL,

In returning his warmest thanks to the Royal Families, Nobility, Gentry, and the Public for the liberal support he has hitherto received, begs to assure his patrons that it shall be his continued study to merit a continuance of their support, by paying every attention to their comfort, combined with a strict view to economy and convenience of those who may favour him with their patronage.

Within a few years this Hotel has had the honour of receiving the patronage of the late Queen Dowager, the King of Saxony, the Prince of Prussia, the Grand Duke Constantine of Russia, and most of the principal English and Foreign Families of distinction visiting this romantic and interesting district. It is situated close upon the Lake, of which it commands extensive views, and within an easy day's excursion of all the principal Lakes and Mountains of the district.

CONVEYANCES OF EVERY DESCRIPTION KEPT.

Omnibusses meet every Train at the Terminus of the Kendal and Windermere Railway, one mile and a-half from Bowness, and Private Carriages if required.

Bowness is within ten and a-half hours of London, four and a-half of Manchester and Liverpool.

Agent to the Lancashire Insurance Company. — House and Estate Agent.

Drawn & Engraved by W Brooks. Editᵈ

WINDERMERE FROM NEAR THE HOTEL

Published by J Garnet, Windermere

HARWOOD'S VIEWS IN THE LAKE DISTRICT

May also be had in Books, very neatly done up in Illuminated Covers.

Books, with Six Views, price 1s.	Books, with Twenty-one Views price 3s. 6d.
Ditto, with Nine, 1s. 6d.	
Ditto, with Twelve, 2s.	Ditto, with Twenty-four, 4s.
Ditto, with Fifteen, 2s. 6d.	Ditto, with Twenty-seven, 4s. 6d
Ditto, with Eighteen, 3s.	Ditto, with Thirty, 5s.

HARWOOD'S DRAWING BOOKS, SOLID SHETCHING TABLETS, AND DRAWING BOARDS.

Manufactured from his Improved Patent Paper.

J. Harwood has great pleasure in offering to Artists the above articles, which possess entirely novel and valuable advantages for Pencil and Chalk Drawing. The ease and softness with which the pencil works, the deep and rich force of colour which it throws out upon this paper, far excels any effect which can be produced upon any other kind of drawing paper, while the delicious softness in the perspective given by using or blending with it their Metallic Pencil, will be found of a character at once to enchant the Artist. — The same delightful effects are produced by the chalk.

Harwood's Sketching Books are made from the best Drawing Papers, and have fine and appropriate embellished Covers.

HARWOOD'S ART-UNION DRAWING PENCILS.

These Pencils are warranted to be manufactured of the best Cumberland Lead, and will be found, upon trial, equal to any that are made. Any of the hard or deeper shades used by Artists are prepared, and each pencil has its distinctive lettering.

Price, Sixpence each.

HARWOOD'S UNIVERSAL MANIFOLD WRITERS,

For producing Letters, &c., with copies in duplicate and triplicate, at one operation; which, for superiority, have gained the approbation of the mercantile world.

PLAIN AND METALLIC MEMORANDUMS, &c.

Sold by Garnett, Post Office, Windermere; Belcher, Bowness; Nicholson, Ambleside; Ivison, Keswick; Hudson, Robinson, Dawson, Atkinson, and Hargreaves Kendal; and all respectable Stationers and Booksellers.

Printed in Great Britain
by Amazon

65526841R00087